*There is existing in men, a mass of sense lying in a dormant state, and which unless something excites it to action, will descend with him, in that condition, to the grave. As it is to the advantage of society that the whole of its facilities should be employed, the construction of government ought to be such as to bring forward, by quiet and regular operation, all that capacity.*

\- *Tom Paine, 1737 - 1809, journalist and political activist.*

*We must not perish by the distance between the people and government, between people and power, by which Babylon and Egypt failed. And that distance can only be conflated, can only be closed, if knowledge is in the homes and heads of people with no ambition to control others and not in the isolated seats of power.*

*- Jacob Bronowski, 1908 - 1974, scientist and historian.*

# Inside

# Adventures in the gardens of democracy

Kevin d'Arcy

First published
in the United Kingdom
in 2017
by Rajah Books

40 Bruce Road
London E3 3HL

Printed by print2demand,
Hastings, Sussex

EDITED BY
MICHAEL EVANS
CHRIS CRAGG
AND TIM CHEATLE

COVER PICTURE BY
ALAN TUCKER

ISBN 978-0-9556706-3-3

BIC categories: JPHC, KNTJ

# The past informing the future

**T**his is how I became a journalist and the crazy world it can sometimes be, but also about much more. It shows how media links people and government. It also shows how people in media can influence reality. As the Canadian Marshall McLuhan suggested, the medium can be the message.

I had worked for years not noticing politics, but over time it became more important, to me and it seemed to everyone else. Journalism was always an important key. It can tell us who we are and where. And journalists are a privileged class, usually knowing what others do not. At the same time, those in charge of our world have been getting less support. They often don't seem to be working for us. They have not changed, but most of us have. Partly because of improving media, but also because we are better educated, we are more ambitious than our parents. The number of people in higher education nearly doubles every twenty years. This is my bid to help close the gap between government and the people.

It was luck that I became a journalist. It was luck that it gave me education. It was luck that it gave me the opportunity to meet the people at the top of their worlds, in journalism and other professions.

It was luck that has taken me round the globe, from New York to Moscow, from Cairo to Mexico, from

Stockholm to Singapore. Having three lovely wives in succession was also lucky, together with many outstanding friends.

In essence, I began by promoting free media and then, by implication, free speech. But somehow this became the promotion of better public involvement in government. If I could do it, why not others? I was not so lucky in changing the world, as much as I tried, or as much as I hoped. There were some successes, some little triumphs, which others might remember when I've been and gone. I offer my record to all of those still looking for a lever.

# A conversation yet to come

## A FATHER TALKS WITH HIS SON

*Do you remember this thing called Parliament, Daddy?*

Oh yes, I do, indeed, my boy. And it still seems just like yesterday. We were all taught about it at school, about Britain having the mother of parliaments, but were still not very sure about that, as were also told that democracy came from Greece, from the ancient city state of Athens.

*Yes, but what happened to Parliament?*

Well it just fell out of use, I suppose, at much the same time as the building that housed it was starting to fall to bits. Once they had moved the politicians out there seemed little point in moving them back, as the nature of their work had changed.

*How come?*

Well, it was all to do with media, I suppose. What had come to be called the public agenda was no longer being drawn up in Parliament, but much more often outside of it. Meanwhile, the proportion of people who were getting higher education, who cared and could understand the issues, was getting bigger every day. And they could not see how politicians were working for them. *They* were not involving *us*. While reading newspapers and scanning the web did not seem to help a bit.

*Explain.*

Well, politicians had formed themselves into gangs, apparently for philosophical reasons, which they described in words like left and right, calling themselves political parties, and then staged verbal wars. They seemed to forget that the House of Commons had been set up by Oliver Cromwell in order to to reach agreement.

*Who's he?*

Oh, it doesn't matter now. But few people could even read back then, so it was inevitable that those who could would have to look after business. But that was all a long time ago and nothing like today. We can read. Nor did it work when I was young. So, very slowly, it gradually dawned, both on people and politicians, that the people's elected representatives badly needed new job descriptions. Fewer people bothered to vote. Over fifty years turnout for elections fell from 84 to 59 percent. Even fewer supported parties. Only one percent were members of parties. So we now elect people to administer policy, while creating policy is the business of the public. Just as in ancient Greece.

*But you said that media had made this happen.*

Yes, well, the House of Commons had for long been made up, roughly half and half, of lawyers and journalists, as they were experienced at describing ideas, but it was increasingly journalists who were not politicians who began to define the urgent issues, in newspapers, radio, blogs, whatever, and the public all joined in.

4

*So what was this thing called the Fourth Estate?*

Oh, son, let's not confuse the issue. That was really ancient history.

# Me and Saint Mugg

## AN ACCIDENTAL START

I should start at the beginning. I left school at the age of fourteen. After the second world war there was no unemployment and sadly a serious shortage of men. So the employment exchange steered me to Fleet Street, then smelling strongly of wood paper and ink, to learn the skills of an office boy. Printing bank notes was my employers' main business, but owning journals that amused the owners was seen as a diversion. One was Punch, the satirical weekly, which was largely known for its place in dusty waiting rooms for dentists around the empire.

Readers usually needed dusters. As older readers grew less able to dust, the owners looked for a livelier editor and settled on a man from army intelligence then sheltering at the Telegraph. His name was Malcolm Muggeridge. He started work the same day as me but made a rather bigger impression. It probably helped that he looked like Punch. It also helped that the sound of his laugh not only removed the years of dust, but appeared to shake the building. The front page of the journal lost its advertisements, replaced by a single cheeky drawing. He insisted on reversing the habit, so deeply engrained in a post war Britain, of pretending that Europe had ceased to exist, especially its intellectuals. He doubted every kind of religion. He shunned the Royal family. This was dangerous stuff for the printers of banknotes, but the attention he got for the journal was sensational. As evidence of his lack of convention, Malcolm persuaded the owners of the office to convert the attic into a flat for the cartoonist Ronald Searle, who already had a house in Paris, to make him more employable. Few would have noticed if it had not been for his companion, a Parisienne straight from one of his drawings, with heavy makeup and fishnet stockings.

Many years later, I was working in radio for the CBC of Canada, in London. They asked if anyone could interview a much older Muggeridge, on his interesting views of life after death. It had been arranged through his son, a lecturer in Toronto. Of course I had to volunteer, if only to clear my head of the memory of a rabid anti-Christian. I drove to Sussex in my Jaguar 240, bestowed by friends who had left for Ottawa, to find the cottage at the end of a dark Sussex lane by the kindness of a candle. I was welcomed by Malcolm and Kitty, his wife, and I immediately reminded him of his earlier convictions and asked for an explanation. It seems he had become a religious expert on television in the USA. He had helped elevate Saint Teresa of Calcutta. He claimed that his memory failed him.

At about this time I had met a Teresa from Hungary who was staying with her mother in north London, who I offered to take for a drive to Kew Gardens. A knock on her front door produced a surprise, the early television superstar Professor Alan Taylor. It seemed he had married her mother. He interrogated me on my future intentions, but also challenged me on my knowledge of Malcolm. Of course he knew more than me. Well, he said so.

I also bumped into Bertrand Russell, the philosopher and mathematician, who lived at that time in Richmond Park, as I carelessly walked up Richmond Hill. I should have apologised, but found it impossible to speak to a childhood hero whose words I had read in the wartime *Picture Post* with absolute fascination. Like Malcolm, he had warned people off religion and I tended to believe him. But he did not speak when I rudely bumped into him. Just stuck out his tongue. Embarrassing me even more, of course.

Malcolm and I worked in different offices, in a building off Fleet Street with marble floors, but still it was certain we would have to meet. It happened on the circular staircase, as he was apparently heading out for lunch. I later learned that the actual purpose was an intimate assignation with Lady Berry, wife of the owner of the Telegraph. This was before his religious conversion. He also believed in interrogation. He demanded to know who I was, what I did, in what I was interested. On learning I could play the piano he ordered daily reports on concerts and, soon after that, on plays, in the style of *The Times* and The *Daily Express*. He ignored my pleas of ignorance.

I doubt now if any if the reviews were published, but it was hardly surprising if, after that, I developed an ambition for greater things, so wrote the same letter to eight leading British critics on how to get their jobs. In those days

8

being a critic brought glamour and fame, they were the philosophers of their age. (I had seeped myself in Bernard Shaw, and explored the US with Alexander Woollcott and George Jean Nathan, as well as Dorothy Parker.) Seven wrote back at considerable length, in style very close to their typical output, flaunting fulsome knowledge and sense of self. The eighth responded with a single sentence, the only one who answered my question. And he was the one who was still employed long after the others had faded away. His name was J W Lambert. His succinct advice I still remember. 'Dear Kevin, success in anything depends on being in the right place at the right time, as well, of course, the ability to seize opportunities, as and when you see them go by.' I now call that Lambert's Law, one of the few I still respect.

# Standing to attention, almost

## INSPIRATION IN THE DESERT

**p**unch was interrupted by national service. Every 18-year-old man who wasn't disabled was subject to two years of boredom in the hands of sadists officially called sergeants, who were skilled at enforcing obedience. I was ordered in training to keep my head down, as 'a dead solder is a useless soldier'. I have certainly remembered that all my life. It has often come in useful. Then I had the choice of clerking or driving and I opted for the second, for open air and a chance to learn a new skill. Some weeks later I landed at night on freezing sands and was told I was in the Sahara desert. I spent time touring a fragrant Egypt in a powerful, unmilitary Humber Hawk for something called Field Security. I seldom had to wear a uniform. I was encouraged to grow a beard. I stayed in some grand hotels. When confined to barracks I thought it would be fun to add to official bulletins a fake dispatch called Part Three Orders with bizarre inventions of regimental disasters. I pinned it to the notice board. Even senior officers appeared to approve. Journalism had clearly begun. I was destined to meet people from all walks of life, culture and nationality.

Because the Suez invasion was not called a war, nobody was awarded medals, despite the loss of lives. I was occasionally drafted to other war zones, but always ended up in Moascar (meaning camp), largely avoiding enemy action. I was knifed once, before shooting my attacker, but the medical orderlies I swiftly fled to fainted, so I discovered how to look after myself. Shortly after, non-knife bearing Egyptians taught me how to play squash rackets with skill, but poorly, later, against the comedian Spike Milligan.

After national service I took any job that had a need for my slender talents, mainly in clothing trade journals - *The Outfitter* edited by Mr Woolley, *Men's Wear* by Mr Cotton and *The Tailor and Cutter* by Mr Taylor. John Taylor started a consumer monthly, *Man About Town*, bought by the property man Michael Heseltine. I later followed, to join *About Town*, which then was trimmed down to *Town*. This was the first post war journal exclusively for men. Heseltine moved to bigger things.

*Town* employed some brilliant people. Gerald Scarfe, the cartoonist was one. Jeffrey Bernard, the drunk, was another. Jeffrey was always ill, of course. Gerald never lost an opportunity, when later interviewed on any subject, to mention that we were all owed money when *Town* magazine was closed. The politician Michael Heseltine very wisely never replied.

# Know how

## IN THE COUNTRY, COMING UP

**S**oon after I found myself in Bournemouth, helping to edit a society weekly with the pretentious title of *savoir faire* (unpronounceable by Dorset locals, who preferred to call it saviour fairy). The wealthy hunting, shooting and fishing set were thought to be hungry for social recognition, being not glamorous enough for the London glossies, so society weddings and the like were seen as bait for filthy lucre.

I ran a column which attracted praise from a Fleet Street star columnist called Hannen Swaffer, who nevertheless thought my own 'pen name' not credible. Running out of cash, the magazine was inherited by the printer, who asked me to run it as a glossy monthly, so we went upmarket with lots of fashion and a handful of famous names. One of these was Cecil Beaton, the celebrated designer and society photographer who insisted that, if I featured his house, a Stuart hunting lodge in the shire of Wilt, he would have to insist on supplying the pictures. I demurred, without mentioning money.

A maturing moment was when I met William Connor, the Cassandra columnist for the *Daily Mirror*, after a local recording of the BBC's Any Questions, during which he had been almost totally dumb, when I put a question to him at the local pub, to which he had invited the studio audience. He paused, and stared, and asked my age. When I told him I was twenty he replied 'You sound like a man of forty'. Ouch. Connor was famous for his forthright views adroitly using arcane English words to replace merely implied expletives, which were banned in the working man's *Daily Mirror*.

Richard Drewitt, who sold our advertising, later joined the BBC and became the producer of the nation's best chat shows, with Michael Parkinson and the rest.

Bournemouth, incidentally, was the stage for my first romance, with a Romanian beautician for Elizabeth Arden. She was related, she said, to King Carol of Romania who was living then very close, in Poole. Which could make her a princess.

# High society, writ large

TOWNEND, FELLOWES, THE KRAYS AND BOXER

The next stop from there was to *The Tatler,* still stumbling along as a social journal, reporting on high life all over Britain, where as features editor I produced bizarre pieces about people I barely knew. Harry Fieldhouse was the editor then, known for his soft suede shoes and addiction to old cars. My essential source of information was the social editor, Peter Townend, whose encyclopaedic knowledge of the upper classes so often included embarrassing detail. We had many dinners when Peter would record, with precise green ink, his mischievous suggestions.

Peter revived the debutante balls when the royal family decided to drop them, with the help of his mate Lord Julian Fellowes, later author of Downton Abbey, known to those who may watch television. Peter went on to edit *Burke's Peerage.* This was when I met the actor Peter Sellers when he was pretending to flirt with Princess Margaret. When I met her sister, the Queen, much later I thought it best not to mention this. I later wrote a column on money for *The Tatler,* edited then by the brilliant Mark Boxer. I assumed my readers were never short of cash. Not typical of me, of course.

Mark Boxer had previously run *Queen* magazine and then the short-lived *London Life.* This was the bible of swinging London, where I edited features, with David Puttnam, now a lord, in dextrous charge of art, or layout. It was fun having lunch with the novelist John Mortimer, an unusual food critic badly missed. We helped to glamorise the East End Kray brothers, criminals then feted in smart north London as rather amusing sadists. Mark's cartoons were especially clever as, apart from their intrinsic wit, they were updated versions of Osbert Lancaster, the famous *Daily Express* cartoonist. But, while Lancaster carped at Chelsea pretensions, Boxer targeted Hampstead.

# Setting standards

## WINTOUR, SHULMAN, BEAVERBROOK, COHEN

**M**y actual background had never been a problem. The *Evening Standard* seemed eager to hire me, in the apparent impression that I was a boy from the shires who mixed with the higher social circles where they had probably never heard of weekends. No-one knew I came from suburban Twickenham, born to a civil servant and seamstress. (Although my mother's father, an illiterate Barnado boy, made a fortune out of food.) The *Standard* editor was the famous Charles Wintour, quietly labelled Chilly Winter, another ex army intelligence man who was much admired by the Canadian publisher Lord Beaverbrook for his ability to attract high income readers and, therefore, expensive advertising. Wintour was never keen on talking, unless it was to address his wife as a 'silly woman'. Beaverbrook also noticed me after I had headlined a nebulous review by the Canadian Milton Shulman of an English musical with 'Tinkle, tinkle' repeated endlessly. 'Top rate journalism' his telegram read the following day from the south of France. Wintour's daughter Anna went on to edit the US edition of *Vogue*, while Shulman's daughter Alex ran the UK edition. Not such silly women, it seems.

If anyone was silly, it should have been me. Having left school with no qualifications, my education had now begun. I soon gave up drama (not as dramatic as life) but later won awards for journalism, both in print and radio. I was always learning by talking to experts. I was lucky. I was privileged.

There were others at the Standard who thought they were privileged. Wintour's target of high income readers meant that he staffed the Londoners' Diary almost entirely with youths from Eton and Oxbridge who were said to know 'some people'. Real people had to straighten their words. Another column, London last Night, was directed at a similar set, of rich and naughty and brilliant young things. Except that they seldom were. Many were simply pure invention, honourable this and honourable that, born of an anxious need for copy to justify expenses. The letters column was similarly ambitious. Impoverished peers were slipped some banknotes to allow their names to be fixed to letters on subjects close to Lord Beaverbrook's heart but written by people like me. That was also my education.

Extended lunchtimes at the *Standard* were common. Those with Wintour were largely silent. Others with people like Stan Gebler Davies, surely the most charming of professional Irishmen who could never resist another whisky, would very often last out the day, usually in Yates in High Holborn. A favourite topic of conversation was his aunt and writer Edna O'Brien, who he could never decide if he liked or not. The experimental writer B S Johnson often joined us. I sometimes grasped what was going on.

I also took an extended holiday, in an effort to avoid an unpopular manager. I went to Venice via the Orient Express, then took a boat to the Greek port of Piraeus. I stayed on Hydra, where I met Barbara, my first, American wife, whose father had run the US army airforce during the second world war from somewhere underneath the Tottenham Court Road. In Hydra I met the singer Leonard Cohen, who had yet to make his name. I had also spent time with a politician's mistress, a beautician at the Hotel Grande Bretagne. We had fun avoiding the not so secret police. Her son became a Greek prime minister, which one I now forget.

The Standard was Fleet Street at its best in the second half of the twentieth century. Competition between the afternoon papers was furious and fast, with normally eight editions a day. Nowadays there is only one, I believe. There was the down market *Star* and the mid market *News*, but the *Standard* was definitely top. The competition made the great mistake of covering all London as a single community. The *Standard* concentrated on the centre, both better educated and funded. Direct competition eventually died. The dailies lagged in quality of output. I did my best by enrolling on a course in advertising design at the Central School of Art. Formal training in journalism had not seriously begun, but what I learned at Central about typography and lettering equipped me well to earn good money at designing editorial. I will always remember the advantage in Fleet Street of being one of the few journalists admitted to the sacred print room, to be able to check the shape of pages by reading the metal lines upside down. It always helps if you drink with your colleagues.

Another course in the psychology of colour has often come in useful. Print design had previously been left to printers with a 19th century mechanical background. I stole ideas from the US and Europe and gradually helped to improve presentation. I started on the Standard and worked my way through a number of the national media. Again, it was largely luck.

# The rising Sun

## JAMES CAMERON AND FRIENDS

y next step was to The *Daily Herald*, at that time owned by the Trades Union Congress as the principal voice of the Labour party. They had agreed to sell it to the Daily Mirror, then sympathetic to the Labour movement, who announced they were changing its name to *The Sun*. I assumed there would be a rush of talent but, when I arrived, discovered to my horror that I was the only new member of staff, as features editor. At the age of 24, this was especially daunting because most of the staff were twice my age. Many were considerably older.

The other problem was the plan for re-launch. The publishers surveyed newspaper readers, to discover what they liked about the papers they read. The new product offered matching content. This overlooked the simple fact that there was, therefore, no clear incentive for readers to change existing loyalties; a clear example of how not to use data. It was fated to end in British tears. It was sold to the (then) Australian Rupert Murdoch. Meanwhile I felt like a boy among men, impressed by their airs of self assurance. The gossip column, Henry Fielding, was edited by a scintillating man who seemed, on the face of it, not suited to the work. Alan Hall was a bon vivant, with a sharp wit and a fondness for wine who may have never seen a pint of beer. He graduated to the *Sunday Times*. His side kick, Alan Dick, was of similar cut, with the added gravity of having reported from Spain from the centre of the civil war. He had lost a lung in the crossfire.

Long lunches for Hall were golden periods, spent in the Long Acre Carlton bar, assisted by wafts of fine champagne and visits from sympathetic hacks like war reporter James Cameron. James had been sacked from every paper for always refusing to follow orders. Never the less he got major scoops, like witnessing the very first nuclear bomb test and helping to found the Campaign for Nuclear Disarmament. These lunches were not wasted time. The gang always returned before copy was due, boisterous with reams of unlikely stories which I managed to make fit. James slept after lunch in our only arm chair. But how anyone thought that this flippant stuff was appropriate to a socialist paper had always left me utterly dazed. Even without the help of champagne. (Alan's favourite response to insulting letters, of which he had more than his share, perhaps, was 'There is a lot of truth in what you say'.) Senior editors had weightier problems. Nobody seemed to care.

My only memorable contribution was an account of persuading Vidal Sassoon to cut my hair, as possibly his first male client, which persuaded him to adjust his business. Alan Hall retired to France, he said to give lessons on tasting wine. No idea what this did to his prose.

# Nearly new Nova

## FIELDHOUSE, WAUGH, FROST AND HAYES

After the *Sun* came *Nova*, aimed, it said, at intelligent women, apparently rejecting all women with emotions. It was the first major women's magazine since the second world war. It was the brain child of Harry Fieldhouse, for whom I had worked at *The Tatler*. I had previously tried to interest the publishers, ahead of the US launch of *Cosmopolitan*, to start a woman's monthly called *Freedom*. After *Cosmo* took off on both sides of the Atlantic they instead bought Harry's title of *Nova,* as a new star on the British block.

I was invited to join as managing editor with a totally unspecified budget, setting records for spending not since surpassed. We recruited Auberon Waugh as a start. Evelyn Waugh, his father, had scribbled for *The Tatler*.

Upperclass young Waugh was sent to Butlin's Holiday Camp, which was a straight steal from the US *Esquire* when they dispatched the elegantly suited Tom Wolfe to report on the basic delights of Broadwalk. Such was the birth of New Journalism.

I enjoyed the visits from the media mogul David Frost when he came to see the proofs of his monthly column. He always welcomed me warmly when introduced, apparently forgetting we had met before, also that I wrote his column. By that time I had written for big US journals like *The Ladies Home Journal,* edited by the adroit John Mack Carter (the Aberfan disaster was a major story, as most recovery money had come from the US), *Holiday,* run by the great Ted Patrick, and *Esquire*'s smooth editor Howard Hayes, who had published many of the world's top writers, but also used Brits to add cheekier input, such as lists of the greatest boors. My hardest task for *Esquire* was profiling the playwright Tom Stoppard, the first author to have two plays on Broadway. Stoppard insisted on interviewing me. I fell back on his family and friends. *Forbes* and the *Institutional Investor* were also good to work for. Being paid in big dollars was a boost to the ego. I bought my very first car.

*Nova* made a lot of noise and attracted attention for journalistic bravery, mainly because of the design by Harry Peck, who had learned much from *Twen,* the avant guard German magazine created by Willy Fleckhouse. But the constant problem, never resolved, was its masculine domination. It is true that most editors in the 60s were men, while now they are more often women. Nova's first colour pictures of childbirth were typical of its masculine bias. Women, in fact, did not like to see this. The intimacy was too extreme. Hence, there were more male readers than female. Not an advertiser's ideal.

# Going it alone

**T**hen followed a period of busy freelancing at a time when media seemed to boom. Commercial television was growing, but so were glossy magazines, in pursuit of similar advertising. Newspapers also launched magazines, with John Anstey at the *Telegraph* jumping in first. Writers and editors were in demand and were being paid serious money. In a single day I could commute between shifts: on *The Times, The Telegraph,* the *Financial Times* and prosperous magazines like *Farmers Weekly* and the much less prosperous *Freight News.* Editing a venture capital journal for a while was instructive, if not so immediately useful. I designed Viewdata for ITN, for news in text via television, and we launched before the BBC. I ran a business news broadcast for the *Financial Times,* revised several times a day, for transmission via BT phone lines. I designed the very first issue of *Penthouse,* wittily (I thought) using the font named Venus. The joke went unobserved.

Incidentally, Bob Guccione, the founder of *Penthouse,* was a US citizen of Sicilian origin who had made an impression at the *Daily Express* as a flattering photographer of beautiful women wearing equally flattering clothes. But he realised that *Esquire* and *Playboy* no longer pulled men and, with the help of Harry Fieldhouse, still editor of *The Tatler,* decided to major on women minus clothes, albeit romantically lit. This was during the swinging sixties, when social norms were quickly changing. The English stiff upper lip was relaxing daily, the British renaissance was beginning to surge.

(The BBC, as the moral arbiter, still repressed subjects like sex and gambling and, by implication, even talk of earning money. It had not been long since BBC staff were sacked if they got divorced.)

Flyers were printed promoting *Penthouse*, but delivered only to reactionary conservatives, as a way of levering credit from printers to launch the magazine; outrage in the House of Commons was predicted and reported. A copy of my dummy front cover, soon after delivered to the *Sunday Times*, pressed the button to start the presses.

Bob admitted to me in his Chelsea apartment that the title of *Penthouse* had little meaning in Britain - penthouses were not yet a British thing - but his long term plan was to launch in the US without having to face a head-on clash with the established competition like *Playboy*. This succeeded in making him, for a while, one of America's richest men, with the biggest town house in New York. There was no denying that the use of politicians as publicists was canny. On the other hand, I have yet meet anyone to compare with Bob in talking so much and saying, generally, so little. He thought that, with black coffee and exercise, he should live forever. He was wrong. He died early of cancer.

I was asked to profile a property developer for *Vision*, a European monthly. He took us to court to stop publication but, thankfully, failed to do so. His promotional target was the USA, where he planned to buy a bank but was not well enough known without written evidence. Gerald Ronson undoubtedly talked a lot but said nothing of substance until (he thought) we had finished. He then expanded into boastful mode, explaining how he had broken the rules while doing a deal in Paris. He had pressed political buttons. After the   interview he got someone into *Vision*'s printers and found I had used the revealing truth. I flew from Paris to defend the case. The judge in Dublin where the journal was published luckily refused to support him. After all, I'd recorded the meeting. But it got us good publicity. A few years later he was fined £5m for conspiracy, false accounting and theft and committed to a year in jail, if for quite different and bigger offences. But having a criminal record did not exclude him from invitations to Buckingham Palace, under the umbrella of working for charity.

Profiling the playwright Tom Stoppard for Esquire was challenging, as he dextrously preferred to interview me. I made do with his friends and relations. It was even harder with the painter Bridget Riley, who made it plain that she distrusted words. The result was a doctoral thesis, almost.

Occasionally I would get a commission to completely revise the editorial for rich but faltering specialist journals, including the presentation. That was welcome news for my bank. I thought I would get the care of my former home, *The Tatler,* to be beaten at the post by a radio reporter, Libby Purvis, who proceeded to just about last six months. The publisher had the grace to apologise and confided that he'd almost appointed me when I claimed that Mona, my new wife, was Britain's most beautiful black woman. Too late. I'd moved on.

# The not really Private Eye

## DEEDES, FOOT, HARTWELL AND PAULSON

The *Telegraph* group was a comfortable base. For a while I did duty on the *Daily Telegraph* diary page, edited then by (Baron) William Deedes, who was the easiest person I have ever worked for, despite his distinct, patrician style. He had a gift for reassuring everyone, an essential part of leadership. *Private Eye* made 'Dear Bill' a figure of fun when they found he was friendly with Denis Thatcher, the husband of the prime minister. They may not have known that his early years were spent with an uncle in Bethnal Green, one of the poorest parts of London. He travelled only by public transport. He knew the common man.

Then I met Paul Foot. Paul had more influence on investigative journalism in Britain than anyone I have known. He also had more class. There are two ways of understanding that. The first is that he was born upper class in every cliched, conventional way. I first met him at the *Sunday Telegraph,* where I was in features and he on the diary, appropriately called Mandrake (a poisonous plant). As we walked the corridors towards a liquid lunch, the commissionaires, all former soldiers, who were common fixtures then in all of Fleet Street, duly clicked their heels together and gave him a smart salute. My eyebrows obviously asked 'What the hell?' as he quickly explained that he blamed his father, Hugh Foot, as the last governor of Cyprus and, as Lord Caradon, the British ambassador for six years to the UN.

Paul, born in Palestine, grew up in Cyprus and Jamaica and went to what we British call public schools. The first was Ludgrove in Berkshire, the second was Shrewsbury in Shropshire. He described them both as pretentious and absurd. After national service (in Jamaica, courtesy of his father's influence) he went to University College, Oxford, where he was meant to study law. However, together with old mates from Shrewsbury (Christopher Booker and Richard Ingrams) his energy was mainly directed at producing the satirical *Parson's Pleasure*, the precursor to their finally (almost) grown-up journal, the fortnightly *Private Eye*.

The *Eye* took over from Muggeridge's *Punch*, just as *Punch* had mimicked the French *Charivari*, but with a much more savage and political slant. Many would describe it today as one of the most important media in Britain. A fair number of its reports have turned out to be wrong, but a sufficient number have been enormously influential, especially those published in the back of the book, which was for many years the special responsibility of Paul Foot. He will be remembered for freeing The Birmingham Six and his defence of the man charged for the Lockerbie bombing. There was also the famous Poulson affair, with T Dan Smith, in the city of Newcastle. Smith was the leader of the Council, Paulson a London builder with the ear of the Prime

Minister, Harold Wilson. They were extremely generous with taxpayers' money in building the Venice of the North, as they called it. I contributed to that report.

*Private Eye* was bought soon after launch (and lunch) by the comedian Peter Cook, who poured thousands of pounds into it, if only to meet the frequent costs of appearing in court to defend the legal actions against the many scurrilous stories. John Wells, Claud Cockburn, William Rushton were other outrageous stars of the paper, but Paul was always the sober one, attending editorial meetings in The Coach and Horses with not so much a joke and a glass, but simply with paper and pen. Paul, however, spent most of his life trying strongly not to be upper class. This despite his conspicuous, if polite, self-confidence which is commonly confined to public school boys and despite his clear, stentorian diction which is normally also equally confined. This made him especially useful in radio. His uncle was Michael Foot, briefly leader of the Labour party, and both had similar vocal styles with unstoppable delivery.

The best explanation for Paul's inner drive might be found in his first real job, at the Glasgow Daily Record, where he was won over by strong, working class left-wingers with logic on their side. He soon became a member of the International Socialists, the precursor of the Socialist Workers Party, to which he was loyal all his life. He would say it is important to understand that they had no truck with autocratic Communists, just socialism as it should be. While in Glasgow Paul received lascivious open postcards from the poet John Betjeman's daughter Candida (later Lycett Green), whom he had described as the most beautiful woman in England, inviting him down to 'the country' for the weekend, all of which were eagerly read aloud by his colleagues. It must have been the first of many awkward problems he managed to survive.

Later I was making a family affairs documentary for BBC Radio on the dangers of riding motorbikes and thought it could be useful to get some advice from an experienced, non-metropolitan policeman, so made a date with Sussex HQ in Lewis to interview a sergeant. Arriving on time, I was nevertheless locked in a room for an hour before a senior officer arrived to fiercely interrogate me on my 'relationship' with Paul, who, of course, had no reason to be liked by the many policemen whose criminal incompetence he had demonstrated over years. Finally, if reluctantly, I was allowed to do my job, but the sudden realisation that I had my own police record, also that Paul was mentioned in it, cast a new light on my relationship with authority. I think I was impressed.

When working at the Telegraph I had been summoned by Lord Hartwell, the publisher, who had been told by his wife of a piece I had written for the US *Atlantic*

*Monthly.* It was an analysis of British politics. *The Sunday Telegraph* had just been launched. He put me on the staff. *The Sunday Times* gave new birth to investigative journalism, so the *Telegraph* felt compelled to compete. *The Sunday Times* had an apparently unlimited budget, courtesy of the Canadian owner, Lord Thompson, which was a resource very hard to beat. It became an ever more pointless battle and the day came when a number of *Telegraph* reporters saw little point in carrying on. After everyone else had decided to leave I picked up a copy of *The Economist,* always on my desk but seldom read, and immediately applied for a job. My stay there was not so long, but fundamental to my professional future and understanding of democracy.

# The ivory tower

## BURNET, CALLAGHAN, MACRAE AND STEVAS

'Y ou and I, Kevin' said the editor 'will be the only journalists on this newspaper. All the others are politicians manqué or economists manqué.' That editor was Alastair Burnet and the newspaper he was talking about was *The Economist,* which many people would describe as a weekly news magazine, but never mind. The label he preferred indicated the stress he expected in the writing. This would never be a laid back look back at the world, but ever looking forward to the world as it could or even should be. I dare to suggest that *The Economist* now has a greater influence on the behaviour of government, in the UK and elsewhere, than any other media in Britain.

The flattery Alastair offered was well received. In his view employing experts was essential, but still of very little value if they could not make contact with the readers. From my point of view I had applied to join after a frustrating period of earnest slaving in the corridors of, first, the *Daily Telegraph* and, next, the *Sunday Telegraph,* subject to an old-world form of leadership usually dubbed as amateur but often described as foolish. I later discovered that my work for the *Atlantic Monthly* had been edited in Boston by the son of the Liberal leader Jo Grimond, John, who was now on the foreign staff of *The Economist* and who could say whether he had needed to rewrite it. Thank goodness he had not. I was charged with reporting on home affairs, which meant everything that happened in Britain outside of Westminster. I took over from the slightly precious Norman St John-Stevas, who went on to be, among other things, an acolyte to the memory of Queen Victoria and a minister for Margaret Thatcher; although I still remember Norman's break with Thatcher, when he reported that 'Margaret always says what she thinks, but does not always think what she says'. Again, throughout my time at The Economist, Alastair never touched my words. For the first time, after years as a journalist, I was allowed to feel responsible. It was also good to see, after publication, Economist stories being followed by others, often in every media.

At the start, I was to follow the work of a former editor, Lord Geoffrey Crowther, as he established a couple of royal commissions; one to reshape local government, the other to launch the Open University. To watch him at this work was to witness a brilliant mind, which I attributed entirely, if generously, to his journalistic training. In 1969 my brief was changed to cover the new problem of Northern Ireland. ('You are Irish, aren't you? said Alastair, and I thought it best not to disagree, so spent several months hoping not to be noticed as a reporter in an inflammable province.) Quick religious conversion was very necessary. 'My father was catholic' or 'my mother was protestant' rather weirdly always worked. Here I was suddenly made aware of the influence of The Economist. Whatever suggestions I made for solutions were swiftly tested by James Callaghan, the minister in charge. But all I was doing was trying to make sense of briefings from such as senior civil servants, who relied on the anonymously written Economist to never name its sources. On the spot conversations I mainly remember for the eagerness to talk of the past, a more careful need to talk of the present, but almost total refusal to talk of the future. Tradition can be obsessive.

Nevertheless, the unique aspect of Alastair Burnet was that he was a master of television as well as print. And his character suited both admirably. Gravitas was a word that could have been created especially for him. Strong, considered, informed, kind, and worldly wise. His craggy Scottish face spelt experience: slightly pock-marked, often flushed by familiarity with malt whisky, but with a firm and friendly gaze. While his voice, with its lowland Scots burr, offered nothing to dislike. He often thought best while prostrate, but sober, on the floor.

Editorial conferences at *The Economist* took place first thing on Monday morning, high up in the editor's office at the top of the ivory tower, purpose built in St James's Street in London's west end. Across the street was the conspicuous office of Apple Corp, the publishers of Beatles music. (Conspicuous because of the big green apple.) Our office had been partly designed by the staff and was the first

London office with air conditioning. From the very big windows we could look down into the back gardens of both St James's Palace and Buckingham Palace, which seemed to provide something of a moral advantage. Even the royal corgis could be seen from above, subservient, as befitted their position. Everyone at the conference was expected to say what they expected to deliver for that week's edition by no later than Wednesday evening.

On my first week I was not asked, but was given three stories to do, plus the possibly more important task of filling everyone's glass with whisky. This was at ten on Monday morning. Alastair's deep voice suggested that perhaps I had been a wee bit too generous with his whisky. That was the only criticism I ever had from him. Certainly on Wednesday evening, when everyone was hitting their typewriters hard, Alastair's principal task seemed to be to carry around hampers from our local grocers, Fortnum and Mason, replete with game pies and quaffs of champagne, while calling out encouragement. Our glasses were always full.

Alastair made clear on my very first week there that 'I don't expect to see you in the office on any day but press day, Wednesday. The real world is out there, not here'. I can't imagine hearing that from any other editor, especially nowadays when all information is expected to move from computer to computer and anyone not seen sitting at his terminal is thought to be wasting time. Talking to people has gone out of fashion. Unique information has lost its edge. But being at the *Economist* for me made taking lunch at the nearby Little French Club, the former headquarters of the French resistance and the think tank for the wartime British Lion Films, considerably easier. The time spent there with the food writer Fay Coventry, later Maschler, and the author Julian Barnes must have helped my English, if doing nothing for my French.

If I contributed anything to *The Economist*, apart from some sensational reports of local government corruption which I had been unable to use on the Telegraph (never question the middle classes, old boy), putting many city councillors in jail, I would say it was, as Alastair had expected, the ability to focus the attention of the reader. Short, sharp sentences in standard English are now a reliable norm in the paper, but before then were much less known; this not only in the *Economist* but also in every other so-called serious newspaper. I happen to feel that this directness, together with a confident grasp of the subject, is the hallmark of what is certainly one of the most important journals in the English language. Or The University of Journalism, as Alastair preferred it.

Alastair increased the paper's circulation during his term in office by 60 per cent, and its influence by many times more. And this was all made possible by the strength of his personality. (That is, on top of the massive advantage of being in legal control of the whole publication, superior to all other directors, an advantage shared only with the editors of *The Guardian* and *Financial Times*.) One of Alastair's keenest students, Andrew Neil, a fellow Scot, wrote 'Working for Alastair was a master-class in journalism – with fun thrown in'. Neil was quite a master himself. As features editor he argued the case for briefings, meaning deeper than the normal short reports whenever the subject deserved it. I wrote briefings on media.

All the same, Burnett was private, a bit of an enigma. I knew he loved horse racing, but he hated to see them jumping, as it led to so many fatalities. Obviously as a joint creator of Independent Television News, he loved news bulletins, but if you entered his office unannounced he would inevitably be shouting insults, in either a Scots, Irish or Welsh accent, at the television. Which might have surprised anyone who had previously only seen him in his sober, responsible onscreen persona. He was fascinated by politics, but would toss the daily invitations to become a politician directly into the bin. He would welcome senior politicians and diplomats to our weekly in-office lunches with gracious condescension, giving the strong impression that he had every sympathy for their doubtful points of view.

Many newspapers have these private lunches, but *The Economist* lunches created an aura that lifted them well over the rest. Alastair was keen on cricket, if only because his cricket mad father had sent his mother from Edinburgh to give birth to her son in Yorkshire in the hope that he would be able to play the game for the county. But Alastair's game was really the world. Even beyond the world, as he guided television viewers through every stage of the first moon landings, almost as if he was there. He explained elections to the television public with supreme authority, plus the Falklands war and two royal weddings. He admired the folksy American television presenter Walter Cronkite. Cronkite must have had a liking for him.

Alastair faltered towards the end of his career, by accepting an invitation, no doubt with a tempting financial hook, to become editor of the rapidly declining *Daily Express*, but it was clear that he did not grasp either the actual nor the potential audience. Neither did his long-term right hand man George Ffitch. He refused a payoff and went back to Independent Television News, to help make it, yet again for a while, the best news channel in Britain.

What this period in my life meant most to me was to witness the ability of a single individual to master more than one profession, written journalism as well as broadcasting; an example I was keen to follow.

It would be wrong not to mention other members of the staff who made the Economist so important at the time. Two stand out especially. Norman St John Stevas I have already mentioned, and Alastair delighted in frequently teasing him for his purple shirts, his purple ink and his camp behaviour (otherwise known as his Roman tendencies), not to mention collecting Queen Victoria's knickers. But when Norman became leader of the Commons he brought in what he correctly called 'the most historic reform at Westminster in the 20th century'. This was the system of select committees, where a group of members from every party, uncontrolled by the party whips, could question ministers and civil servants on their ways of doing business. These began work in 1980 and today everyone can see their value. As the son of Spyro Stevas, a Greek hotelier, it was obvious that the former journalist, The Lord St John of Fawsley, had forced a Greek advance in British democracy, demanding value for money. He had also gained an amusing PhD at Oxford on the subject of obscenity.

Less known, but no less important, was the deputy editor, Norman Macrae. He was little known for a number of reasons. One was perhaps *The Economist*'s style of not normally identifying its writers, although some of his more substantial pieces, usually supplements tacked onto the paper and written always with a personal flair, were credited to him alone. His views were strong but always unconventional. All the same, his subject, economics, as a former Treasury man, put him at the heart of the paper, where he stayed for forty years. His intellectual powers were phenomenal.

Macrae forecast the creation of the world wide web and the increasing access to information. He also forecast de-nationalisation, the collapse of Communism and the rise of

Asia. A survey of the US produced an order for a thousand extra copies for the White House. He was bold enough to suggest that until the US solved its race problem it could never sort out its economy.

The fact that few remembered this was entirely down to Norman's modesty. He courted no public attention. If you challenged his stand he would simply giggle. His command of language was also surprising. He coined 'stagflation' and 'intrapreneurship', possibly 'privatisation' and 'Eurocrat'. But working with him needed special skills. He could think much faster than he managed to talk, so that when Alastair asked him for his plans, his jumble of mumbled words were usually interrupted with 'Great, and how much space would you want?' The final result on Wednesday evening was always pellucidly clear. This was partly down to his ageing but loyal secretary, who claimed to be able to read his writing, scrawled in pencil across a lot of paper.

Although apparently an expert on the world of technology, Norman was famous for losing fights with simple things like fax machines. And he rarely used a telephone. Explaining his importance to potential journalists was always hard to do. Nevertheless, the emperor of Japan sufficiently recognised his understanding of Asia to award him the Order of the Rising Sun, with Gold Rays. It is not known if Norman giggled.

It was at *The Economist* that I discovered Switzerland

and for the first time doubted the function of democracy. Having left my first wife, I met Teresa, a Swiss model in Bond Street, who invited me for Christmas with her family in Basle. While there, enjoying the snow and the schnapps, my journalistic nose for stories suggested I explore this magical country. The relationship of government to the people seemed remarkably effective. Doors opened with speed at the mention of the *Economist* and I returned to London with a torch named truth. Alastair was not enthused. The Swiss are not like us, he said. He did not think it worth a mention.

# Sound news

## COOKE, LEE, TUSA, STUART AND DE MANIO

**W**orking so closely with Alastair Burnet made me hungry for a bigger platform than print. After all, Alastair spent as much time on television, presenting moon landings and various elections, than he spent in the Economist office itself, but he had experience of doing that for years. I had been reporting on the growth of radio - new local stations were to cover the country - and sensed that here was an opportunity that needed to be seized. I had always worshiped Alistair Cooke and his magnetic, mid-Atlantic voice.

I started with the first local station created by the BBC, in London, and worked my way up the network from there, through the domestic and world services. I was lucky in my timing, as the corporation was trying hard to shed its Oxbridge image and my accent was undeniably Middlesex. Other graduates were David Walter, who became political editor at ITN, and Michael Vestey, the diplomatic star and columnist for *The Spectator*. Both had the nous to nose for news and to notice the way the wind was blowing in the national agenda. But it must be said that David complained that ageism hit him at the age of 40, which is why he had left the BBC, and Michael sometimes gave the impression that property prices were his main motivation, and he did own a lot of property. But Michael's book on journalism, *Waning Powers*, in fact demonstrated just the opposite. It caught exactly the fishbowl obsession that often takes over at the BBC.

More quietly, in the background (as well as living next door to me) was the studio engineer Brian Eastman. He transformed my report on the Mafia in London by running the Mahagonny music by Kurt Weill in the background. He went on to a glorious production career in theatre, film and television, notably creating Agatha Christies' Poirot, Jeeves and Wooster and Porterhouse Blue, echoing his time at Cambridge. He now prefers California.

For me, starting at the BBC, once mechanics were overcome, meaning dextrous editing with razorblades and tape and remembering how to be kind to microphones, the rest was not too hard. Most recruits to local radio were 'resting' actors and would-be disc jockeys, whose understanding of current affairs was, to put it politely, slender. Writing scripts was not much much different from writing anything else. Writing tightly for the *Economist* was little different from writing more tightly for radio. That was in the 1970s.

I soon learned that, if I was prepared to work at hours and on days when others were reluctant, editors let me to do what I liked. This included major documentaries which might not have attracted major audiences, like the Mafia controlling the London casinos, (which the Gaming

Board very soon closed down), but were very useful at getting attention from producers on other networks. I also found that, working as a freelance, there was a growing market all over London, like the British Forces Broadcasting Service and the Central Office of Information, then Capital Radio and LBC. And writing stories for magazines meant that I could use the material again. Sometimes magazines would ask me to repeat my reports on radio. And vice versa. The COI I most remember for seeming like an army division, with soldiers correctly sitting at attention, plus a serious devotion to rank appropriate to its war-time origins. The COI produced propaganda programmes for the British Information Service, used by embassies abroad. British excellence was the key.

Very soon I was providing material for sequence programmes on Radio Four, as well as the BBC World Service, which sometimes included trips abroad, such as a posting to New York. Which is where I met Alistair Cooke at the BBC studios in Rockefeller Center. Cooke was seen as the BBC on both sides of the Atlantic. Although born in Blackpool, he became American, nevertheless later accepting an honorary knighthood. I stopped him in the corridor on a Wednesday evening, on his way from recording his weekly Letter from America, which he had delivered faithfully for seventy years. I told him I was there because of his example and asked how to get his job. 'I am never going to retire, young man' he said 'so you are going to have to push me off a bridge. Failing that, you could try your hand at putting out a letter from London'. He had started by doing that himself, albeit for the NBC. And so I tried, but it did not last long. Comparisons, as someone has said, are odious.

Perhaps the oddest experience during this time was going to a Foyles literary lunch at the Dorchester hotel, with the brief of interviewing Wilfred Pickles on his long life at he BBC, and finding sitting across from me the widow of Richard Dimbleby, for many years the most famous broadcaster, who asked my advice on what to do with her second son, Jonathan. 'As you are a journalist, you ought to know. At the moment he is living in a tent in a field and wearing the most awful jumpers.' I don't think I was very helpful.

Of course, working for the BBC does not mean that you are member of its staff. Possibly most content, then and now, is provided by outsiders on various contracts. I was always a freelance. Once accepted as a reliable contributor, commissions just rolled in. By offering my best interviews to Pick of the Week, making me I think the most frequent contributor, I made sure that every producer knew me. As a freelance I could choose my programmes and times, without being a slave to others' deadlines. It was easy to avoid dull programmes. And I preferred to work for generals, not corporals. As long as my commissions were delivered fit for use, I could take a holiday whenever I liked. And I did that all the time. The main problem at that time was payment. Unions organised annual staff pay rises, but freelancers were ignored. The most successful freelance, John Tusa, who had presented every major news programme, one day realised that all presenters were freelance, so suggested we used that power to strike. We did, and took over the BBC boardroom. Live programmes were in instant chaos. The director general arrived in ten minutes and immediately gave us what we wanted. Tusa went on to run the World Service and the Barbican Centre, no doubt still as a freelance.

At about this time I was living in Chelsea with a girl I had met on the ferry from France who was appealingly sick for the whole of the journey. I had to feel paternal. She was beautifully dressed and beautifully undressed and we lived together of a couple of years until she took up acting. Sarah Cooper was good at languages and her father sold cars and so of course she could drive. This was very useful when I met the author Laurie Lee, a close neighbour, in the Queen's Elm pub in the Fulham Road. (His most famous book, Cider with Rosie, had introduced a generation to the magic of the British countryside.) Laurie was moaning about being asked by his publisher to retrace another of his books in which he had discovered Spain. 'I can't drive and I've lost my Spanish' he said. The Today programme presenter Jack de Manio was sitting beside him and asked what he thought might be the solution. Not surprisingly to anyone who knew him, Laurie said 'A beautiful girl, who can do both very well.'

Jack invited him to the BBC and Laurie described his needs very clearly in his winning way on Today. About a week later I met Laurie in the pub and asked him if the wheeze had worked. He invited me to inspect his flat, barely big enough for more than one. It was totally full of Post Office sacks with applications from thousands of women. 'What am I do to? he said. Soon I was waving Laurie and Sarah goodbye on their literary adventure. They were pictured on the front of every newspaper. Laurie was a famously charming man. I soon needed another girl friend.

For a while I paired with a young Polish blond whose father was an attache at the London Embassy and who seemed to be practising to become a honey pot, as they put it in diplomatic circles, but she disappeared at much the same time as some unconvincing tv license inspectors appeared en mass at my door and asked to see my licence. As they must have known, the time I took to find it was enough to create a key for the door. They next day I came home to find that my flat had been carefully dissected. I assumed they were Brits, not Poles.

Another Chelsea neighbour was the actress Joyce Grenfell, she of the brilliantly inspiring monologues, who surprisingly knocked on my door one day to warn of a water overflow pipe she had seen from her bathroom window. She often popped round for tea after that, as I happened to notice that her performances were very similar to the American Ruth Draper, whose recordings I had played so often. She pleaded guilty, but explained the reason was that Draper was both her aunt and her heroine, so she felt she had the right.

There were few subjects I did not cover in radio; farming, religion, science, politics, psychology, the law and so on. I am proud of helping credit unions to get under way in the United Kingdom by explaining their expansion from post war Germany to most of north America. While a long spell on the BBC news desk was a useful place to watch news being processed. I filled a dustbin every hour with pathetic press releases.

While reporting on science I struck up a friendship with the secretary to the BBC science editor, who suddenly appeared on television delivering the midday news. This surprising me, partly because I had been away in Sweden, but also because she was the only member of staff with an emphatically dark skin. Moira Stuart told me later that this was the only reason for the offer. (She was used to people looking in at the office door and saying 'Oh, nobody here then'.) The only other black people on staff were either cleaners or cooks. She did not like it but needed the money. She was uncomfortable, as well, as a public figure. A fierce moral campaigner, Mary Whitehouse, was a member then of the BBC trust, and had insisted that someone with a non white face should be put in front of camera. Moira had no journalistic experience, essential until then for every news reader, but had an obviously perfect command of English, which was not surprising considering her education at one of the top schools for girls.

Moira became the BBCs most most popular television presenter, at least until she touched her sixtieth year, when the management bravely decided to shift her. The furore in the popular press continued for a considerable time. The strange fact was that Moira in the studio was better known for her Jamaican patois (no sweat), and to me for her addiction to all night parties, not always so correct. She was nevertheless a dream to be with, as everyone who worked in the BBC said, always appearing to be in control - until that was taken away. She has since been more modestly tasked with reading the news on Radio Two.

A shadow hung over my radio days which I did not know until much later. Radio London was my first connection, where a fellow reporter was a very quiet girl who was interested in my days in Greece, because she planned to make a trip for stories. We shared an occasional coffee. She never returned and I forgot all about her, as journalists generally change their plans at the very shortest notice. Twenty-five years later I discovered a book written by Richard Cottrell, a former television reporter who had been elected to the European Parliament and it told the story of Ann Chapman's murder. I took it, even then, as a personal loss.

A man had been convicted but Cottrell was not convinced by official reports, so used his powers as an MEP to conduct an investigation. In essence he blamed the CIA, as Ann had appeared to have become mixed up with the US promotion of the military coup in Greece, to foil Russian designs on the Mediterranean. The convicted man was released from prison, but the actual murderer was never discovered behind many layers of official confusion; from the Greeks, the US and the British. The body was returned to London, but her parents were prevented from seeing it. Again, no explanation. The idea that people in charge of governments were possibly not quite up the job was very much reinforced. Much later I made a trip of my own, to my second wife's home in the north of Malaysia. We were going to be married in a Hindu temple, but I thought it would help to pay for the trip if I did some radio reporting.

My future father in law, a Malaysian magistrate, helped to pull some official strings, which was quite an achievement, as the BBC had not long before been banned, in a political tit for tat. Margaret Thatcher had raised fees for foreign students, so Malaysia, which was totally dependent, took it out on the Corporation. All the same, I got interviews with the nation's founding fathers and returned to London as pleased as punch. However, it clashed with the Falkland's war and radio space was suddenly limited. What I had thought were firm commissions from producers were withdrawn. I was seriously out of pocket. And furious. The BBC had lost its halo.

# Transatlantic soundings

## STAROWICZ AND BROOKS

The solution was another example of luck. I knocked on the doors of the nearby studios of the Canadian Broadcasting Corporation and discovered what was probably the nicest club for freelancers in London. I also polished my mid-Atlantic accent.

Canadian culture nicely bridges the gap between the US and the European, producing still an attention to detail but, if you like, wearing jeans. The main driver for this at the CBC was Mark Starowicz. He was born in Britain of Polish parents but moved very early to Canada. He had a gift for ignoring conventions, in terms of subject as well as treatment, in both radio and television, and so becoming, in my opinion, Canada's most important journalist. He was a champion of the nation. Living under the shadow of the USA, national identity is important to Canadians, including those who speak mainly French. Americans see Canada as the place to go whenever they feel uncertain.

CBC people always laughed at my jokes, even when I had not made one. Studio interviews were never liked as much as chats with people in the street. Mark described his ideal of radio as television without the pictures. No doubt, when he moved to television, the ideal was reversed. And of course the CBC paid in dollars, which always seemed much bigger than pounds. I understand now that the climate has changed, but I found that working for the CBC was, compared to the BBC, considerably more human. I felt even more at home in my posting to Toronto, but a law was due to make French compulsory in Canada and, mon dieu, French lessons had always failed me, so there seemed little point in staying.

But another stroke of luck came along. A new journal, the *Financial Weekly*, agreed to a survey of broadcast media and the way they reported business in Britain. I slammed into radio and television news, pointing out their misunderstanding of finance and their lack of commercial nous.

This was picked up by Radio Orwell, a local station, and they asked me to mend that gap with a popular educational series to be offered nation wide. The Right to Work was a thirteen-part series that was used by every commercial station and won the Society of Authors annual award for discussion and current affairs. It basically explained how the world of work works. It was pretty serious stuff. It had an influence on a lot of media, encouraging a wider reporting of business, in place of simply investment and finance. I polish the award at regular intervals and try to forget that the comic Nicholas Parsons was chosen to present it. Donald Brooks, the Orwell manager, kindly at the Savoy Hotel, covered my clear confusion.

Another award, from John Deere Intercontinental, for business reporting in print, was presented by a member of the House of Lords who seemed mainly interested in Mona, my second wife, then wearing her brightest sari. Yet another award, from the European Commission, was possibly the most important, not because it was for reporting Europe, but because it came in the form of a generous cheque. Of course I thought warmly of Europe.

# Venturing into Europe

## HYDE, HODGSON, MANSELL AND PRESTON

**R**eporting on Europe was not my choice. It was simply that the *Financial Times* could not decide if the subject was important, or important enough for the paper proper, so asked me to produce a newsletter on the subject, *Community Markets*, to help to test the response. I had just launched the newsletter *Chemical Insight*, the first industrial sector (and highly expensive) bulletin in Britain, for my old friend Michael Hyde. Advertisements at that time brought little income, so relying on subscriptions made sense. Michael grew from being an underpaid editor at the family owned publishers Benn Brothers to a multi-millionaire when, years later, he sold his golden egg. Nobody else had his expertise. He got what he deserved. Subscription paid media now looks like the future. It is already the principal funder.

My apparent expertise on Europe attracted the attention of other old friends. Paul Hodgson had run the BBC French language service and, on visits to Brussels, had joined with other hacks with similar briefs from other countries. They realised that the Common Market had no strategy for dealing with journalists, so volunteered to take the lead. Thus the Association of European Journalists was born. His son, also Paul, I had worked alongside, and he successfully drew me in.

It was not long before I became UK secretary, about the same time as I had started work in financial public relations. The City of London was fast expanding and there was a desperate shortage in the PR business of people who understood finance. The pay was tempting and I was pleasantly surprised to meet PR people with real skill. Up until then I had shared the opinion of most journalists that the profession was a waste of time. PR resources then came in useful in encouraging outstanding guest speakers. For over two decades we had a procession of famous people to meet the media at private lunches with leading journalists, first at the elegantly Edwardian St Ermin's Hotel, then at the more austere London offices of the European Parliament. There was hardly a minister, ambassador or chairman turning down an invitation. It is obviously extremely useful to oil the wheels between government and media. And not only to politicians.

The only consistently disappointing guests, ironically, were ministers for Europe. Although Ian Duncan Smith made quite an impression by appearing to almost break into tears when questioned in a polite but challenging manner. Everyone was confused. And a US ambassador, a retired general, insisted on lecturing us on the geography of his country, despite everyone at the table having worked and lived there, some writing outstanding books.

Members of the AEJ included Edward Mortimer, who became a spokesman for the United Nations, Bridget

Kendal, who became master of Peterhouse, Cambridge, and Quentin Peel, the FT foreign editor who later moved to Chatham House, the foreign affairs think tank.

In 1992 the AEJ met in London for its annual conference, at a time when many former Soviet countries had applied to join the European Union and the British section used two hotels and the QEII conference centre to host 400 leading journalists. Central to success was the charming Gerry Mansell, former managing director of the BBC World Service, a genuine multi-national. Also essential was Roger Broad, both Paul Hodgsons and the older Don Hatwell. Don had been secretary of the AEJ before me. Funding came from institutions, like the Foreign Office and the Bank of England, together with major British companies, and a hundred speakers had been engaged to talk on government and media. There were lunches and dinners and receptions for days and a lot of serious talking. It was the first AEJ conference not to make a loss. There were also nice surprises. Such as the Foreign Office saying that wine at their reception was unfortunately out, due to the pristine white marble floor, so we would have make do with champagne. The biggest disappointments came from spokesmen from Brussels who were asked for advice on accessing information. Their answers were basically little more than 'We'll tell you when we're ready'. We wondered why they had come.

As UK secretary it became my duty to attend central

meetings of the AEJ which, with English as my native language, progressed to representing the association at intergovernmental meetings. Brussels and Strasbourg became familiar, plus a number of other capitals when a delegate from the world of journalism became relevant at many debates. We gained official recognition not only at the European Union and the Council of Europe, but also at the OECD and UNESCO. This made obvious the need of governments to work with journalists, the better to engage with public opinion in designing legislation. Attending meetings also worked to our advantage in helping to co-ordinate policy with other media organisations.

This was during the eighties and nineties, when I also joined the International Press Institute, always led in Britain and sometimes centrally by Peter Preston, then editor of *The Guardian*. He has always been known as a man of principle. He once suggested that the only laws that mattered were all in the Ten Commandments. Through the IPI I was sent as a delegate to a number of sector-specific meetings. I had become a peculiar kind of diplomat. Not bad for a kid with no education or comfortable private income. Luck.

I was often puzzled by other journalists, speaking for mainly national pressure groups, when they supported campaigns against concepts like hate speech, which seemed to simply target opinions with which they couldn't agree. I soon grasped that many saw their job to be promoting the political parties that pay them. Loyalty was the flag they carried. On the other hand, a Foreign Office minder expressed surprise after I had spoken at a conference in Warsaw when I told him over dinner that self-policing by journalists was absurd. At the conference I had said the opposite. I explained that, like him, I was not speaking for myself, but for the policy makers of the IPI. Yet in reality, I pointed out, that if politicians cannot police themselves and, especially, if police cannot police themselves, it was naive to think that journalists could. A media court was the best solution, with independent judges.

Overseas travel brought other benefits. In particular I got perspective on how other nationals looked at Britain and particularly our media. Being British seemed to earn a respect that took me time to understand. Indeed, I could not understand until I discovered two major figures. One was Tom Paine, the 18th century journalist who authored the pamphlets *Common Sense, The Age of Reason* and *the Rights of Man*. These inspired republics like the US and France, but they also showed how to use standard English to reach the common man. Only the bible outsold those pamphlets in the English speaking world. A fuller account is in my book *Who's in charge here?* which was largely inspired by Tom Paine. The other figure was Brendan Bracken.

# Dear Brendan

## CHURCHILL, KEYNES, WAUGH, ORWELL, PRIME, GOEBBELS

t is impossible to appreciate the unique shape of British national media throughout the twentieth century without recognising the very personal contribution of Brendan Bracken. His name was given to Bracken House, the home of the *Financial Times*. Very few remember him now and I have only lately discovered him. The reason for the pre-eminence of *The Economist* and the *Financial Times* over other British newspapers lies in their almost unique tradition of editorial independence, where the editors have the final word. Brendan Bracken controlled each paper and decided from the start to ensure this, so that the core product, information, is shielded from other interests. *The Guardian* has similar protection, enforced by a charitable trust.

Brendan Bracken also ensured that, during the Second World War, the BBC stayed independent, despite the plans of Winston Churchill, as prime minister, to control it. The BBC is technically not part of government, but its royal charter is administered by government on behalf of the British throne.

Bracken was largely self-invented. In reality, he was born in County Tipperary. His father died when Brendan was three, which must have had an important effect on his

60

clearly chaotic childhood. His mother gave up on him when he reached fourteen and sent him off to an uncle, a priest, in Australia, after which he became even wilder, yet apparently educating himself. Which was when his second life began, with no acknowledgement to the past.

He returned to England at the age of nineteen, pretending to be only fifteen, and paid for a place in a noted public school, Sedburgh, absurdly claiming to be an Australian orphan, the result of an unfortunate bush fire. At the end of one term he had achieved his ambition, the right to wear a public school tie, which he did, with style, ever after. Two years later he was selling advertising for the publishing firm of Eyre and Spottiswood, being rapidly promoted to publisher and editor. The following year, still fresh from his short spell at school, he was working hard for Winston Churchill in his first attempt to become an MP.

After leaving his briefly useful public school in Britain, Bracken taught for a while in Bishop Stortford and joined the League of Nations Union. From here he moved to London to work for the magazine *Empire Review*. This put him in touch with the editor of The Observer, who introduced him to Churchill. Winston's wife, Clementine, was not comfortable with this intrusion into her domestic arrangements, especially when the body of Bracken was often found comatose on their furniture in the evening, without even having removed his shoes. His calling her 'Clemmie' was another form of excessive self-confidence which she found hard to take. Meanwhile, Bracken continued with publishing. Having founded *The Banker* in 1926 he went on to take over the *Financial Times*, the product of a merger with the *Financial News* in 1945. With the help of an Austrian financier, Sir Henry Strakosch, he also gained control of the then stumbling *Economist*. His passionate interest in the best of journalism was firmly imposed on all his titles, which was not, at the time, the norm. He started modestly by founding *The Banker* and, later, *History Today*. Then he became the MP for Paddington. But all of this was minor stuff. Somehow he became minister of information for most of the war. If anyone guarded the gates of reality for a great deal of the twentieth century, it is clear that Bracken surpassed all others - through his friendship with Winston Churchill.

The politician Lord Longford described Brendan Bracken as the most remarkable man he ever met. His biographer Charles Lysart thought that Bracken must rank as the most significant native Irishmen (although he claimed to be Australian) in English political life since Edmund Burke, who had created the Conservative party.

Randolph Churchill, the son of Winston, described him as the fantasist whose fantasies had come true. Randolph should know this as much as anyone, as it was Bracken's friendship with Randolph's father, before and throughout the second world war, that was the key to his success. It seems that Churchill always called him 'Dear

Brendan', much to the annoyance of Churchill's wife. Churchill valued his ever constant vigour, making up for his own frequent 'dark days'.

Bracken also made his mark on fiction. His contemporary, Evelyn Waugh, put him into Brideshead Revisited, as the fast-talking social climber from the colonies, Rex Mottram. George Orwell, who had worked for him in the ministry of information, used his initials in Nineteen Eighty-Four, BB for Big Brother.

Bracken was also a physical eccentric. With an imposing stature and a bush of red hair, firmly combed to the left hand side, and with what some called almost negroid features, plus typically discoloured Irish teeth, he nevertheless had an assuring manner and apparently total self-confidence. Meeting him for the very first time must have always produced hesitation, so giving Bracken an ideal opportunity to seize the social advantage. Even the bulldog Churchill succumbed, which thus created a special relationship for most of the rest of their lives. Flexing his social muscles, Bracken then moved to North Street in Westminster, which he managed to have renamed Lord North Street (North was the Tory prime minister who had lost America), installing a butler and a cook, retained for the rest of his life. He bought a swanky Italian car, driven by Churchill's former chauffeur. He filled the house with works of art and many pictures of the Churchill family. Stories began to circulate of Bracken being Churchill's 'natural' son.

Clementine was even less happy. Churchill had created a private dining club and invited Bracken to join. A few years later Churchill became prime minister, very largely because of a strategy suggested to him by Bracken.

Churchill had moved from the Liberal party to stand for the Conservatives, where he became Chancellor of the Exchequer. With the Second World War the need arose for a coalition government. But Labour refused to serve under Chamberlain, then Conservative leader, so a substitute was needed. The foreign minister Lord Halifax was selected by the party leaders and Churchill was called to a meeting, expected to simply nod this through. Bracken advised Churchill to listen at the meeting, but to say nothing, voicing no objection, and so offending no-one. After two long minutes of silence from Churchill, Halifax threw in his hand. He could see he had no support. It is true that in previous days Halifax had not been as strong as Churchill in opposing Hitler; so, as others said afterwards, those two minutes probably saved Britain from disaster.

Bracken never joined the Cabinet, preferring posts that kept him close to Churchill. As minister for information, he resolved not to emulate the Nazi Dr Goebbels with close censorship of all media, indeed insisting, against Churchill's instinct, on ensuring that domestic affairs should continue to be freely reported. Providing information, not withholding it, was the better way to control the press, he thought.

This also pleased the BBC. The way in which he maintained a degree of control was less through edict than negotiation, for 'the sake of the wider public interest'. That tradition is largely still with us. Bracken was good with sound bites. He described the economist Maynard Keynes as the man who would be remembered for making inflation respectable. He described Nye Bevan, the Labour politician, as a Bollinger Bolshevik, a lounge lizard Lenin, a ritzy Robespierre, swilling Max Beaverbrook's champagne 'and calling yourself a socialist'. He described General Montgomery as 'a master of caution in all things except speech'.

He was also not without weird habits. He made a show of chatting up women, but apparently just to create social contacts. Most thought he had no interest at all in the opposite sex. Bracken died at the age of 57 refusing all religious rites, despite his Irish Catholic origins. 'The Blackshirts of God were after me' he said, 'but I sent them packing'. There was no second Viscount of Christchurch.

While Bracken's *Economist* has continued to thrive, the FT has had a bumpy progress, apparently unsure of its role as a daily trade journal among its mainly political competitors. Also, along with *The Economist,* it lost heavily in US (and German) publishing; it over-managed its newsletters; it was slow to report barter and countertrade; it chose not to notice Islamic finance; and it failed to cash in on its many awards and its very much plagiarised advertising supplements; while the world's biggest business, trade and transport, could well have lived in another world.

A director I worked with, John Prime, did a management buyout of its overlooked titles covering transport, with an eye on the US *Journal of Commerce*, and made himself a fortune. He also showed how to cut overheads by rejecting advertising, moving the head office from the City to cheaper premises across the Thames (to be followed by the FT) and by moving all data on line. He then set up a charitable foundation for outstanding transport journalism.

# Big Brother's Company

## A QUESTION OF INDEPENDENCE

I also discovered that the BBC had, horrors, imperfections. The recent rash of conversation about fake news needs a bit of perspective. Henry VIII employed a jester to generate fake but useful news. While the BBC has been guilty mainly by default. This echoes Churchill's thoughts on representative democracy: not good, but better than the rest.

Churchill had planned in the second world war to place the BBC under state control ('If Goebbels can do it, so can we'), to be persuaded by his friend Brendan Bracken that feeding good stories to the media was wiser than trying to suppress stories. Ever since, if not before, the management of the BBC has had a problem with their independence. Every government, of any colour, has always complained of BBC prejudice, simply because it tries so hard for balance. This of course means space for critics.

On the other hand, the BBC knows that it is the loudest voice overseas for Britain, so feels it ought to be considerate of governmental policy. A symbiotic relationship.

I once promoted a friend, then a senior BBC manager, to help the Foreign Office at an overseas conference because he had always worked for the corporation, so would instinctively know the proper way to behave at any diplomatic meeting. And that worked out just right.

The downside to this position is the encouragement it gives to anyone in government to lean on the BBC. There is a dedicated department that is skilled at dealing with fractious politicians on many levels, both at home and overseas, but sometimes influence is anticipated so strongly that no pressure is necessary.

An example of this was the strange decision to open a major broadcasting centre at Salford Quays, near Manchester in 2011 called MediaCity UK. The estimated cost to the BBC over 20 years was £20bn. Of course there have always been studios outside London. The stated intention was to more conspicuously lessen the information dominance of the south of England on a national network by moving as much production as possible closer to the audience. This was despite the evidence of BBC surveys showing that audiences did not worry a bit about the source, only about programme content and its relevance to their lives. So the only obvious logic for the move could be the creation of local jobs and boosting the local economy. Not surprisingly, the BBC initially found only eleven people in Salford qualified to work for the BBC, so the 2,000 eventually employed were largely decamped from London. Serious commuting from there to London now seems a permanent fixture. Those who pay for BBC programmes must wonder why they should also be responsible for regional economics. Self-censorship is always a worry. Not many remember that the novelist Frederick Forsyth was a reporter for the BBC who had been sent to cover a conflict in Biafra, Nigeria. The Foreign Office official view was of a small disruption of little importance and the BBC followed along. Forsyth, however, filed a report that the truth was more serious and the result was a diplomatic protest. The UK representative in Lagos flew to London, resulting in Forsyth being recalled and banned from all foreign reporting. The BBC decided that Biafra should no longer be in the news. Meanwhile, planes loaded with British weapons were flying from Gatwick to fuel the war. Forsyth threw in his job and returned to Biafra to meet some missionaries who were eager for the truth to be told. Which essentially was that a trade embargo imposed by Lagos was starving Biafra, including large numbers of children. The story was run by ITN. Suddenly Biafra became big news, so the BBC had to follow.

Another event of longer lasting importance was the problem of Arab-Israeli relations. The BBCs correspondent there for ten years was Tim Llewellyn, who found that his efforts to tell the truth were increasingly getting nowhere. So he also felt forced to resign.

The news that seemed be wanted in London was based on an assumption that was plainly not true: that the Israelis were always being attacked by dangerous tribes of alien Arabs when the opposite was usually the case.

Tim later reported 'That [many] years of military occupation, the violation of the Palestinians' human, political and civil rights and the continuing theft of their land might have triggered this crisis is a concept either lost or underplayed. Nor are we told much about how Israel was created, the epochal dilemma of the refugees, the roots of the disaster. British television and radio's reporting [of the uprising] has been, on the main, dishonest - in concept, approach and execution.'

He quoted a report from Glasgow University that tracked all media coverage for two whole years that stressed the same theme in all reporting, of Palestinian attack and Israeli reprisal, while the truth was nearly always the opposite. It also showed that public grasp of this truth was little more than ten percent. The most likely motivation seems political correctness, forever hovering at the BBC, which is not after all a branch of government, but a public corporation.

The biggest and perhaps most shocking shadow over this legal reality was cast by the David Kelly affair, concerning weapons of mass destruction that nobody found in Iraq. Dr Kelly was a British scientist charged with finding them, but didn't. This was reported by Andrew Gilligan on the Today programme on Radio Four, to the enormous anger of people in government and to the embarrassment of John Scarlett, who chaired the Joint Intelligence Committee and had signed off on the official report that justified the Iraq invasion. A legal enquiry later suggested that the presumably highly intelligent Mr Scarlett might have been 'subconsciously influenced' by pressure from the Prime Minister's office on the final wording of the official report. (Nothing to do with bullying, of course.) Nevertheless, the invasion happened and, after the BBC report, David Kelly was discovered dead in woodland close to his home. Officially this was called a suicide. Evidence was weak.

Pressure was put on the BBC, especially on the board of governors, previously appointed by the government, on an implied charge of incompetence. (By the BBC, not the government, of course.) This lead to the departure of Greg Dyke, the chairman, and director general Gavin Davies, and the defenestration of Kevin Marsh, the editor of Today. All three had records as outstanding managers, so were a major loss to the BBC, as well as to the BBC audience, the owners of the BBC who, of course, were not consulted. The board of governors was also dismissed, leading to no great lament: more dummies were put in place, but only on a tentative basis.

You could also blame the BBC for a practise that has covered the country, what is now called the gig economy. When a director general used management consultants they suggested a way of cutting overheads by employing more labour on a casual basis, so avoiding pay for holidays or pensions. In fact, perhaps the majority of

BBC workers, including the director general himself, were already on a freelance basis, especially most programme presenters. Many BBC producers were surprised when I pointed out that, although always present at Broadcasting House, I was never on the staff. My BBC pass took me all over Europe, regardless of whether I also had a national passport. And journalists all over the world still identify me with the BBC. A wider explanation is in *The voice of the brain of Britain*, my book on Radio Four.

On the other hand, the BBC, as a major employer, has long had a problem with organisation, often making central control too powerful, but often not enough. In my time there, the major problem was the insular attitude of the so-called barons, heads of department who would not work with others. This was eventually sorted out by a vigorous director general.

# Nodding Neddy

## MACMILLAN, THATCHER

t was the eighties when I started with public relations, first handling bids and deals in the City at a time when the financial sector was booming, then running for cover when the boom declined to take a job at the National Economic Development Office, thinking there was safety in the civil service. I had been asked before, but rejected it, as I could not understand the job. My title was head of public relations but, as before, with no job description, which was clearly a basic problem. I was intrigued to discover that Neddy, as NEDO was nicknamed, included the London section of the European Commission's economic and social department, another extremely vague public body. But Neddy's birth was inspirational.

A British prime minister received a vision. He had become distinctly tired of the childish and rowdy behaviour in the House of Commons. Not the right way for gentlemen to behave, he thought. Imagine:

*'All this grandstanding and point-scoring and all for nothing much more than trying to bloody the nose of the chap on the other side, who is out of reach anyway. Surely there must be a better way of taking care of policy. In any case, the slogan of the party has always been One Nation, hasn't it? Ever since the days of Disraeli. Ah, well then, so why don't we have a go at the Scandinavian way with legislation? What*

*they do, it seems, is get a small number of interested experts together in a room to hammer out the major differences before passing the matter to Parliament. A sound idea, even if they are socialists. I think the Frenchies do something quite similar and call it the Economic and Social Council, but we don't need to mention that, do we?'*

So that's exactly what he did. Harold Macmillan was his name and the year was 1962. And - without mentioning the French - he also named it the National Economic Development Council. And it lasted until 1992. And it was a jolly good idea.

What happened was that there were people from each of the three bodies most involved in the economy: the government, the trades unions, the employers. The logo was a triangle, with other triangles inside. There was a big Neddy, which decided on what work to do, and there were a number of little Neddys for various industrial sectors which actually did the work, researching, planning, publishing and so on. The Chancellor of the Exchequer was in the chair, as he had to provide the money. Perhaps Neddy's most significant product was finally getting the Channel Tunnel off (or into) the ground, after centuries of humming and hawing. We also put a lot of work into warning about the growing Glass Ceiling, a major barrier to ambitious women.

The death blow was dealt by an ambitious woman, Margaret Thatcher, the Conservative prime minister, on the grounds that she did not want even to recognise trade unions, quite apart from talk to them. And this was entirely within the prime minister's discretion, as nobody, especially Harold Macmillan, had thought to make it an integral part of government in the Scandinavian manner, only a talking shop in the French manner. (If you don't like one think tank find another. Some know how to behave.)

The end was a bit embarrassing, especially for me as, being head of public relations, it was my job to explain it. Everyone employed there had been made to sign the Official Secrets Act, as we had been recruited as civil servants. But the lawyers finally discovered that Supermac (as Macmillan had been called by Vicky, the *Evening Standard* cartoonist) had been so keen to get the office off the ground that the legal formation got overlooked, so officially we had never existed.

All the same, as an example of running a consensual government, it could still be worth considering. With possibly one improvement. Neddy's triangular logo should have been a square. As academics later stressed, there was nobody sitting at the any of the tables to represent the public.

This is not an official secret, of course.

# Governing what?

## LOCAL MANOEUVRES

In the nineties more domestic interests spilled into my working life. My two young sons were at local schools and my wife volunteered me as a governor. (The biggest voluntary body in the country.) Having escaped committees so far, primarily by being largely freelance, I accepted the role at first reluctantly. But watching the way that business was done, or not being done, by existing governors I moved fairly fast to a central role. As a journalist I preferred to use words to produce action in the shortest time. After primary school I followed the boys to a secondary, where budgets were very much bigger. The realisation that you are legally liable for £14m annually of taxpayers' money makes what might have been a casual decision considerably more significant. Once in position I became more ambitious and found myself elected to chair an area governors' forum; then to be a member of the local schools' forum, where governors and head teachers set budgets for the borough; then as a director of the National Governors Council, with a view across all of England. We enjoyed a lot of lively discussion. Politically, the Council achieved nothing.

The NGC seemed a typical, if grander, version of an average school board. They were broadly divided between amateurs and professionals. The professionals saw themselves as experts, as they had previously been head teachers. Those I call amateur had not been teachers, but some had possibly useful experience of running major public companies. However, the professionals paid little attention to anyone with experience of real life and bullied them unceasingly. The chairman did not intervene. Attending meetings with government ministers was always strictly reserved for the professionals, who seemed to enjoy the tea and cakes and flattery a lot. There was no indication that education policy had even been discussed. More importantly, the NGC's own policies did not seem to draw ideas from its members. But this is the British way, of course.

Despite these limits, the NGC produced fine publications of practical value to all school governors, well designed to guide mainly amateurs through the minefields of educational red tape. However, it is clear that governors are misused. In principle, they represent the public, but there is no clear way to ensure this happens. This has meant that governments, national and local, have been able to play silly games with schools, so that nobody seemed held to account. And of course there have been too many examples of governors falling asleep on the job, in every conceivable sense. But taking local initiative is difficult. It sometimes seems that the most you can do is to dodge the latest guidance. My local council lawyer once explained this by saying that governors were not representatives, but delegates. Ah, so that explains it, then.

Having been an ersatz civil servant, I think I understand the thinking. It is accepted that public input is good, to bring early warning of reaction to policy. And it has always seemed best to meet that gap by involving external pressure groups. But that, of course, is only a gesture, and not a very effective one, either.

On the other hand, in Tower Hamlets we have had the advantage of Canary Wharf, where banks and accountants like to help their neighbours, which has meant that the quality of volunteer governors has always been higher than the national average, experienced in management, as well as finance. This has mightily helped education.

# Clochemerle on Thames

## DOING A RAHMAN

**N**evertheless, decay in democracy hit home in Tower Hamlets. Our local government had long lagged in honesty, while the Labour party had ruled for so long that they were blind to the changing world. Bangadeshis had arrived in big numbers, with little understanding of the British system, but nevertheless eager for group agreement, so were easily persuaded by one of their own, Lutfer Rahman, that he aught to take the lead. They could see that the way he led was traditional. However, it was also quite corrupt, dependent mainly on family and friends - and others only when unavoidable.

Almost the only voices heard against this were those of journalists Ted Jeury and Andrew Gilligan, who (with the help of whistle-blowers) between between them conducted a war of words on the web, as well as in print. The police were contacted, but could 'find no evidence' of the corruption that was obvious. Many said they never looked. Twenty-seven files of evidence had been deliberately ignored. This all grew out of my campaign for the borough to have an elected mayor, mainly through my East End Mayor blog, which led to the bizarre experience of the prospective winner knocking on my door one day and pretending to be a pollster, in order to find out more about me, as I had planned to stand for election myself. It was not the first time he wore a trilby hat indoors with the hope of hiding his identity. He asked fake questions, I gave fake answers.

In the event it fell to one man, Andy Erlam, with three good friends as joint local residents, to take action against the mayor for electoral fraud. They won the case, after four days of hearings and considerable expense. The mayor, Lutfer Rahman, had the use of top barristers, courtesy of the borough's taxpayers. Erlam and his friends relied on a barrister just beginning his career. But they won and the mayor had to go.

The election commissioner, Richard Mawrey, had no doubts. His High Court summary was firm and brilliant. He made it clear that Rahman's evidence was not credible. He ordered him to pay the litigants' costs at once. They claim £1.5m. The lawyers on both sides went into a huddle and agreed that Rahman would hand over deeds to various properties as part of the arrangement. Immediately after he declared himself bankrupt and a veil of confusion was pulled over the properties, which he later said belonged to his wife. No judge could be found who agreed with that but, years later, no debt has been paid.

Private prosecution after private prosecution produced more costs of thousands of pounds, as the nation watched the story unfold over many months and years. So private citizens had taken the initiative and ended by paying the bill. State action was largely invisible. True, Eric Pickles, a government minister, later sent in accountants and government inspectors. But those costs were met by local ratepayers. The accountants were said to have charged a cool million, while the four inspectors were paid £950 a day - until they declared the stables clean. Meanwhile, the new mayor of the borough has cut his budget to meet these demands, to a large extent by laying off staff. The fact that the borough includes Canary Wharf, sometimes called the financial capital of the world, does not mean that cash is unlimited. This is covered in my book 'London's Second City'.

Quite apart from that, I was pleased to be interviewed as a prospective chairman of the local Royal London Hospital. The result was negative, but the retiring chairman offered what sounded like wise advice: not to be seduced by committee meetings, where 'They will only cover you over with paper' but to 'Walk around the corridors and talk to the staff. They'll tell you what's going on.'

However, I had a chance to add some value to borough business for several months as a dignitary at the register office, creating new British citizens. This was originally meant to be a role for mayors or councillors, but over time they stopped showing interest, so journalists were also asked to apply, which is how I first joined in. You need to make a speech of welcome to the borough and to shake a lot of hands. I highly recommend it. To have an audience of a hundred odd foreigners who think it is going to be better for them to be British, and who have saved very hard to pay the fees, would inspire even the greatest cynics to appreciate what they already have. I doubt if there is a better way of making so many happy. On the other hand it has to be realised that immigrants from, say, Asian countries have little experience of saying what they think in public, so inviting them as citizens to consider being magistrates, politicians or even school governors can sometimes seem optimistic.

# Getting the message across

## SPOKESMEN, SPOKESMAN

**N**EDO was closed by Mrs Thatcher as part of her war on trades unions, despite protests from many ministers who found it a useful liaison vehicle, particularly John Major, who was then in the NEDO chair. What I did then was to draw on my experience of public relations in the corridors of government and launch my publication, *Spokesman*. I had been appalled in my time in Whitehall to discover that, despite the reputation of the British Civil Service, the one exception to its admirable standards was the post of the second most important official, the spokesman, or media adviser. There was no job description, no setting of targets, no regular review of performance. This would never happen in the City of London, where clients demand clear definition of what they can expect for their money. And appointment as a government media advisor is casual, to put it politely. A chance meeting in the street can suffice between the minister and the candidate. Reputation, otherwise called gossip, is the process so often used. At the same time, in my role as a representative of media at international meetings, I was constantly asked by civil servants in applicant nations to the European Union for advice on how to deal with journalists in this new free speech society. It was necessary to draw up guidance. I was invited to explain this to the media committee of the Council Of Europe and was surprised to meet a group with a hundred members, together with a fractious Russian, which possibly explains why progress there is so very hard to achieve.

Later I was sent by the Council of Europe to deliver a report on the Soviet Union. The Soviets had exited the Council, not for the first time, on a typical point of non principle, but then, as before, applied to rejoin. The necessary process then was to send in inspectors to check their credentials. I was tasked to inspect the media and its degree of independence. Of course I had to report the truth, being that there was no independence. Indeed, the judge in charge of media monitoring said he had never heard a case, for the simple reason that Russians (you know) have their own ways of solving problems. Of course. It was pleasant, all the same, to drink Jamaican Blue Mountain coffee from Wedgwood china in the Kremlin. Nevertheless, the Russian delegates soon settled back into their Palace of Europe seats as if nothing untoward had happened. The admissions chairman explained the logic. It was better to have them inside the tent than making a mess outside, he said. This is the body charged, as you know, with encouraging democracy in Europe.

Yet institutions such as the Council of Europe, the European Commission, and even the World Bank, were in principle willing to fund initiatives to encourage a free press. I developed a bank of editorial advisers, led by the spokesman for the United Nations, and launched my international quarterly review of policy and media, *Spokesman*. Subscribers came from all over the world, but not as many as I had hoped from Britain; which seemed to reflect the desultory way in which spokesmen were appointed. Then followed a period of acting as a specialist in government working through media. This led to more education in the many ways of understanding democracy. I realised that so-called developed nations themselves have a long way to go.

For example: the scene was a conference hall in Warsaw, Poland, previously used by Comecon, the headquarters of Communism International. It was suitably dark and lugubrious. It had been taken over for the day by the OECD, the Organisation for European Co-operation and Development, for a meeting on ways of improving government. Over the usual drinks and snacks I came across an impressive lady in gold braided military uniform, introduced myself as the delegate for the International Press Institute and asked her who she was. 'I am the US Under Secretary of State for Democracy' she said. I was speechless but, reading my face, she immediately followed up with 'Yes, and I don't know what it means, either' and turned on her heel.

That brief scene is fixed in my mind as a deeply symbolic moment. On one hand I found it hard to understand why a nation that sees itself as the embodiment of democracy would seem to think that it needed a military official to supervise that part of the US constitution. On the other hand, it is possible to understand a nation that sees a need to persuade other nations of the charms of democracy wanting someone impressive to do it. This was before the appointment of a president despite losing the popular vote.

Other western countries have similar schemes, all mainly staffed by ersatz diplomats well accustomed to follow rules. As people they seem very similar. Many have been doing this for decades, sponsored either directly by governments or indirectly by foundations, with the seemingly benign intention of spreading more sweetness and light. They don't get too much media attention, partly because doing good seems dull, but also because they don't want critics looking closely at what they do. Which is nothing very much, in fact.

The collapse of the Berlin Wall was the trigger for western governments to get very keen to help establish forms of government that were finally rid of communism. The USA, with the biggest budgets, set the lead for other democracies to offer practical help to governments who said they were willing to change. Every sponsoring state had the same ambition, to demonstrate how their system was best. Representative government was taken for granted. Administrative procedure was a major focus. The public was rarely an issue. Britain's Westminster Foundation for Democracy was launched in 1992, with the stress on reforming parliaments. The Magna Carta is mentioned a lot, as if this were a demonstration of empowering the people, not disempowering the crown.

The Council of Europe and the European Union were helpful in co-ordinating programmes, without fussing too much about content, such as whether they were fit for use. I played my part, like many others, to explain, for instance, how best to present policy without the need to dictate to journalists, in the standard communist way. But over time I saw that my efforts did very little to improve democracy, as the pathetically underpaid civil servants in those countries swiftly employed their newfound skills to get better rewards in industry. The less talented took their seats.

There were even bigger strategic problems. In 2002 the USA established a camp to imprison and torture in Guantanamo Bay, which demonstrated to the rest of the world that, without trials to establish guilt, human rights could be ignored. Britain's earlier history of torture in Kenya clearly had not helped. Neither policy was approved by voters. The moral ability to lecture others had finally faded away.

The hundreds of workers in the democracy industry all huffed and puffed and insisted, all the same, that their multiple efforts produced results, pointing to the many autocracies that had declared themselves democracies. On the face of it, that was true. Countries quoted were Burkina Faso, Chile, Columbia, Indonesia, Mongolia, Myanmar,

Senegal and Tunisia. A closer look at those countries now would show less clear a picture. Similarly those countries in Eastern Europe which had tied so hard to join the EU, after the need to convince the Council of Europe to underwrite their democratic credentials, look less like democracies now.

The problem was always the process. The wrong people were involved. Heads of state talked to heads of state, government officers to government officers, and deals were done to produce state change alongside others to issue cash aid for various other schemes like arms sales. Nobody mentioned bribery.

This seemed to square the various circles. After all, opinion polls in the majority of countries had shown an appetite for democracy, in terms of holding democratic elections. Only in the most insecure societies, as in parts of South America and Egypt, did people prefer religion or the army. Security was seen as more important. However, it was obvious that the shape of democracy would always depend on interpretation, and the mystic phrase most often used was 'respect for local traditions'. But nobody explained what this meant. Most importantly, that interpretation was left to those at the top of society who had grown to believe that the system they'd been running, which had kept them in comfort for many years, was really not all that bad. Understand the changes as token.

People were allowed to vote, but for nothing very much; mainly for one big beast or another, always promoted by special interests. And once in power the winning candidates would listen first to those who had sponsored them. The creation of policy, the essence of government, was largely done behind closed doors with those same special interests designing the menu. After all, this was normal life for those born into communism.

To western governments, such flawed democracies seldom present especial problems. Cynical academics in eastern Europe describe this as encouraging 'stabilitocracies', which is not so good for them.

Shortly after Warsaw I was dining with a friend, Irina, the former editor of a Bulgarian daily, then political advisor to her president, on a boat on the Rhine with other journalists, to be joined by a man with many attendants with bulging armpits and identical suits, the president of Albania. Irina welcomed him warmly and we spent the evening exchanging bright banter in clear, impressive English. The following day he appeared at our conference and delivered the most impenetrable speech in communist English. He invited questions and I drew attention to the only phrase I managed to grasp, 'responsible journalism'. I asked him to whom they should be responsible. Albanian journalists laughed quite loudly. He did not laugh. He did not answer.

This may seem shocking, but we should ask ourselves if this is really so very odd. Autocracy always looks like democracy to the people who are put in charge. Surely truth in developing nations is no less a truth in ours.

Influence in developing countries is much at the mercy of hidden forces. And so it is in ours. The ability to influence policy must surely be the right of all.

# Goodbye to gatekeepers

## HELLO TO GATEKEEPERS

The delicate dance of governments and media varies both by time and culture. Journalism is but a small part of media content. Most of media is just moving words and numbers and pictures from place to place, lacking context, lacking meaning, usually lacking truth. Scepticism is an essential tool when handling government information. Trainee journalists are often taught to ask themselves in interviews 'why is this person lying?' Of course, most people don't mean to lie, as what they say they believe to be true. As it is, from their perspective.

An extension of this is the belief that spokesmen do very little else but lie, which is equally unbelievable. On the other hand a head of the Foreign Office was quoted as saying to a journalist 'You think we lie to you. But we don't, really we don't. However, when you discover that, you make an even greater error. You think we tell you the truth'. [If not the whole truth.] And when a head of the Civil Service was giving evidence, in an attempt to stop a book's publication, he had to admit to defending counsel that he had 'been economical with the truth'.

I had a similar experience when interviewing a Lord Chancellor in Strasbourg on a point of law when he answered by saying 'I have no knowledge of that'. Only after did I see his intention: that he chose to have no knowledge of that. And when scientists say they have found no evidence of something it does not mean that this something does not exist, only that they have not found it. These nuances must be handled with care before being passed to a wider public.

There is also a problem in trying to tell people anything that they do not want to hear, as they are often reluctant to listen. For instance, I once found myself sitting next to a man conspicuously dressed in hairy brown tweed, better suited for the 19th century. We were at the presentation of the British Council's annual report. The Council, of course, is charged with promoting British culture, which includes the English language.

The man next to me was Michael Wolf, co-founder of Wolf Olins, a design consultancy which has improved the appearance of a number of British institutions through a keen awareness of culture. The Council director was explaining that their regular survey of world opinion had shown that most foreigners believed that most inventions came not from the United Kingdom but from the USA. So their policy for the following year was to do their best to correct that. Wolf shot to his feet and shouted 'You must be mad. People admire Britain because of its traditions. So why on earth should you stop that?' The director mumbled some sort of reply and went back to his script.

The first lesson here is that the director did not want

to hear such a basic truth, so chose to ignore it. The second lesson is that Woolf tried to deliver the message in such a way that ensured it would be rejected. The third lesson is that Wolf's advice (don't tell people what they don't want to hear) was clearly not advice that he followed.

Another problem with communication is that because we all talk every day we can all believe we are good at it. Shortly after the first Gulf war I had an invitation to go to Paris, to join a conference on government and the media. It was a great trip and the very first time I had travelled on Eurostar, first class of course, and stayed at the hotel George V. And the food was fantastic. The conference was rather different. It seems that the Ministry of the Armed Forces was feeling just a bit confused. For the first time in living memory the French media was not content with taking official statements and using them as directed for the sake of the nation. They had instead seen foreign tv reports and decided to follow their line. How could the ministry deal with this?

A large number of foreign editors, from north America as well as Europe, were asked to speak on this issue. When it came to my turn I simply asked if they had not employed professional people to handle official information and, if not, I suggested they should. The serried ranks of gold braided officers made many detailed notes.

Some months later I was again in Paris at a meeting of the Council of Europe and found myself behind a

Frenchman also rich in much gold braid. I introduced myself and told him about my previous visit to Paris. 'Ah good' he said 'well, in that case, as I am the man who was given that job, you might tell me how to do it'.

He may have been joking, but I suspect he was not. Asking a soldier to become a spokesman, apparently without any training, was what you might call very bold. But many spokesmen for British prime ministers have also been appointed just because they were journalists. The normal civil service rigour of panel interviews and background checks are ignored in favour of asking a comparative stranger if they fancy doing the job. For a while this was called (very softly) sofa government. Knowing 'the enemy' is not enough. You must also know (and understand) your 'friends'.

All the same, it was occasionally good to see enthusiasm. After the atomic disaster of Chernobyl, I joined a meeting of the World Health Organisation in Denmark, called to lay down useful programmes to help prevent repetition. Lack of communication had been a big problem for several weeks, making the damage worse. I drafted guidance on proper practice in the event of any similar problem. Later, in Italy, another UN body, the World Food Programme, gave a similar presentation and issued copies of my Copenhagen guidance, exactly word for word. I thanked them. Imitation is nice.

The best spokesman I remember at 10 Downing

Street was called GOD, or Gus O'Donnell. And the reason that he did the job so well was not because he knew so many journalists, but because he knew how government worked, as well as the process of media. The general public seldom saw or heard of him, the secret of his success.

The best strategy I have ever heard came from the nearly forgotten Malcolm Muggeridge. In the second world war he was in military intelligence in Africa before foreign reporting for The Daily Telegraph. He engaged critics for Punch with the strict instruction, 'I don't want facts, I want the truth'. Which applies to all communication, surely.

# Civil civil service

## CUDLIPP, ECKHARD

I have spent some time suggesting ways for governments to improve the delivery of messages. The reaction of officials to external advice is always polite and normally positive. It can be very flattering to see how quickly their antenna sprung to life.

For instance, there was Mexico City. The event was a meeting of delegates from countries belonging to Mercosur, the emerging South American free trade bloc who had been invited to meet people from the European Union to learn from their experience. I was co-chairing a seminar on government communication with an official from the Commission.

I had already sent an edition of my journal Spokesman that had spelt out who did what in Brussels, which I arrived to find translated into Spanish and bound as a book for the meeting. Not bad in under a week. Luckily, to avoid repetition, I had also prepared a mock wedding speech. I congratulated the hundred-odd (mainly male and mainly portly) government officers in the room on their engagement and wished them well for the future. But I warned them of likely problems. Such as believing that technical agreements between them would then solve all their problems. Such as not predicting the public reaction, which could be very emotional. It might all end in tears, I said, if not an immediate divorce. (Brexit was still out of sight, of course.)

The meeting seemed to finish well, judging from the response of regional journalists who had obviously enjoyed it. Indeed, I was reminded of it a few days later at another conference in Britain, at a Foreign Office think tank called Wilton Park, when the Mexican Ambassador to Britain caught me in the bar in a break and said 'You must be the man who gave the funny talk in Mexico'.

It was hard not to be flattered by five minutes of fame, but I was also reminded that serious messages can sometimes be fudged not only by language, but also by style. Was I a comedian or was I serious? I had hoped I was being both.

Wilton Park still makes this pertinent. It was first used during the second world war as a place to interrogate captured enemy officers. After this it became a place to help restore Germany, inviting world experts to offer ideas, so avoiding the disaster after the first world war which had fed straight into the second. Prime Minister Winston Churchill saw that history held lessons.

There are still meetings there on similar themes, mainly civil servant to civil servant, but very few on the essential issue of working with the public. The issue was partly resolved after the second world war by enlisted British journalists like Hugh Cudlipp, later editor of the *Daily Mirror*, creating the precursor in Germany to *Der Spiegel*, called *Die Woche* (This

Week). *Der Spiegel* (The Mirror) survives today.

The subject has recently been revived in Britain with the creation of what used to be called the Nudge Unit. This government section has now been part privatised, or sold off to the civil servants who designed it, and renamed the Behavioural Insights Team. It makes annual profits now of £1.72m, after charging a daily fee to clients of up to £3,800 for advice. The Cabinet Office (the taxpayer) owns a third of it. With the admirable aim of improving the ways that government and others deliver their services, they involve a range of experts. Doing the same, but better, is the theme, including (surprise, surprise) communicating more effectively. All the same, responding to public need seems, as usual, marginal.

There has been a torrent of words on delivering policies, at conferences, in books, in training videos, but seldom reference to a dialogue with the public, the only way to win public acceptance. Encouraging the elite to talk only to each other makes government more distant.

An essential aid to understanding the relationship of media to government could be The Reuters Institute for the Study of journalism at Oxford University, which produces a wealth of international data.

Insularity is at the heart of it all. For instance, I was asked by the Bank of England to apply for a post at the International Monetary Fund, as potentially the first non-civil servant to work as head of external relations. When I met the current director he took offence when I suggested that the IMF was sending out more data than journalists could handle. There is such a thing as too much news, I explained, but some find it hard to admit to self-importance and the IMF had got used to being a US fiefdom. Yet a week spent exploring Washington, the IMF and the neighbouring World Bank, was certainly not a waste of time. For instance, I think I understood much better how international bodies survive with mainly unwritten rules. It helped that my senior advisor for *Spokesman* was the spokesman for the United Nations, Fred Eckhard.

# Who can we believe?

## BLACK, MURDOCH, YELTSIN, ENGLISH

**A** strong memory of my time at The Economist was watching the editor open his mail and scoff at yet another invitation to stand for political election. 'Don't they realise that I have more influence here than on any backbench in Parliament?'

Good government without media simply cannot happen. Government and the public need to communicate, that is nowadays understood, and the function of media is to handle that process, but the problem starts when communication is seen by government as only one way. This usually happens when those in power think they have to decide for everyone. Most public resistance starts here.

The next problem is whether to believe the messenger, who also has the power to distort or, as he would put it, interpret the message, either to make it more relevant to the public, or else more entertaining. (You will notice that many journalists on television now talk about 'the show'.)

Of course the business of government is complex and few would hope to grasp it all. But journalists believe that they should at least try, and they divide the work between them. The public is normally glad to accept this, especially if they know the reporters, so feel that they can trust them. While politicians are also glad, for very similar reasons. They are more glad now than they used to be. Working for BBC radio in the eighties, after persuading a politician to talk, the process was laborious. I had to collect a key from a hook on the wall behind the news editor's desk, walk from Broadcasting House to St Stephen's Green, just across the road from Parliament, to a studio big enough for a desk and two chairs, and unlock the door for the interview. Afterwards I reversed the process and returned the key to its hook.

Now a block right next to the green has a lot of multimedia studios, where MPs will gather in crowds in the hope of being interviewed. There are usually more than are sitting in the House. This is possibly a sign of a change in their priorities. Or very possibly not. This is the heart of the Westminster Village and politicians might be getting more attention, but is this the same as support?

Journalists are rated low among professions, but this compares ironically with the ambition of journalism coming top among new graduates. Which suggests they are ready to face dislike if they can still be influential. But this is just their opinion, of course. Simply because the job excites them does not prove that all journalists have influence. Of course the media can help set agendas, but the evidence that this works its way through to action can vary day by day.

One reason for this variation is the little known truth that most news stories do not originate from journalists, but communication specialists. There are many more of these than journalists and most of them are better paid, so its a profession that attracts the ambitious, not to mention the often very cunning. Most politicians and public bodies have media advisors to help connect with the public and this is where a battle of wits is continually taking place. It is the instinct of journalists to always suspect that the information they are given is doubtful. Media advisors are paid to find ways to deal with that suspicion. There are advance news diaries drawn up every day, to help to separate major stories, although a natural disaster can spoil the best plans.

There has been a considerable growth in news providers in the past few years, in the form of a number of so-called think tanks. These are usually assumed to be independent, but inspection of their funding can show the opposite. Warning notices are often ignored. Facts can turn out to be fiction.

Media advisors have their limits, especially if they call themselves media managers. My Right to Work radio series, with over a hundred interviews, was achieved without any press office help. None of those contacted chose to respond, too busy chasing their tails, perhaps. However, industrial leaders were keen, the moment I made direct contact.

And news delivery is changing fast. Two thirds of people get primary news on-line, rather than from traditional media, three times as many as ten years ago, but thankfully the preference across all age groups is for traditional media web sites. This preference is even greater when background information is needed. So-called social media can not be dismissed, but all news starts from a very few sources, which media advisors always use and which others rely on for accuracy. Two of these are the BBC and Reuters, the British news agency. (*The Economist* and *Private Eye* are my favourites for insight, not forgetting the *New Yorker*.) It is also worth noting that political attitudes are normally formed fairly early in life, usually in the early teens.

All media has influence beyond its target. Beyond the first audience there is always a secondary, including social media. The BBC's Radio Four, for instance, despite its relative small audience, is followed closely by other media, which extends its influence all over Britain and to editors worldwide. I stressed in my book *The voice of the brain of Britain* that although Radio Four takes only 2.2 percent of the BBC budget it still costs more than other radio stations can afford, in Britain or anywhere, which is largely why competition has failed. News providers also prefer the most influential platform, especially when they are asked to provide a broadcast interviewee. And Radio Four, I like to believe, is the most influential media in Britain, setting the lead for all of the others. Editors and politicians are addicted.

Mind you, stories placed in marginal media can be 'discovered' by national journals, so effectively grow extra legs. News providers know this well, so use marginal media to plant the seed of a story whenever they think they can. I helped to launch a new merchant bank with the help of the editor of a financial newsletter whom I knew that news editors trusted. He covered their ignorance of financial systems to explain why the initiative mattered.

And the nature of media shapes the news. The maximum number of words available on broadcast and texted media also limits the amount of background, so often there is none. This reduces the ability to present reports on issues not already understood. ('Explosion in Macau, not many dead'). News providers know this, as well.

More concerning than fake news has been the growth of pre-news, when politicians take two bites at the news agenda. Sadly, journalists succumb to this, despite the danger of boring the public with pointless repetition.

The quality of news depends on the reporter and his ability to extract information. I was once sitting in the highly glazed Kensington *Daily Mail* offices beside the Head of BBC's Radio Four, listening to Chief Rabbi Jonathan Sacks giving a talk to senior editors. The Radio Four head raised his hand to ask a question, which was unfortunately of the kind usually asked by young journalists, not to produce a useful answer, but to boast of their credentials. The Rabbi stood up from behind his table, walked down the room to confront his questioner, then said 'You are the head of Radio Four. You are the intelligent person in this room.

What do you think is the answer?' Ugh. Different journalists have different skills. Some time later the hapless questioner found the peace of an Oxford College.

The marriage of government and media seems convenient, and appears to work best when neither partner is diverted by other interests. To others it can seem inclusive and blinkered. Especially as it is centred on London, convenient for the principal partners, already self-important. Others compare it to the Stockholm Syndrome, where the captive increasingly identifies with the captor, oblivious to all outside the circle. Many editors then convince themselves that the prime minister's trousers are of major importance, above all wars and famines.

So what does this mean? Being careful with the media. And deciding: is it reinforcing convictions, or moving beyond convention? (What you want to know? Or need to know?)

For instance, *The Times* was the most respected paper until it was bought by the Australian/American Rupert Murdoch, and the *Telegraph* was the most trusted paper until it was bought by the soon-to-be-imprisoned Canadian Conrad Black, while the *Daily Mail* is not what it used to be since the death of David English. He was the first to see that women would adopt an increasing role in British society, so acutely steered his paper towards them. He was also the man I sat next to in Moscow, exchanging bets on how long Boris Yeltsin could stand upright without another vodka. A few days later David himself passed on, although through natural causes. I would rather not mention the Express, once the world's most brilliant paper. Relevant to them all is the major challenge of enabling reporters to talk to people, so reducing dependence on information provided only online.

At the end of the day it has to be admitted that the status of traditional media is falling as fast as political loyalty. In just two years the under 35s have stopped using papers and television as a first news resource by roughly 20 percent. (Although they still use their websites as a confirming source.) They are much less keen in being told what's important. They much prefer to decide for themselves. Which is also how they think about government.

# The royal family

## SO JOURNALISTS CAN CHANGE THE WORLD

his is the story of Harry Evans, the boy who made good from Eccles, and his wife Tina, who made good from Maidenhead. It is also about democracy.

The origin of journalism is keeping a journal, which is clearly a personal initiative. And the principal way it concerns other people is if it affects their lives. There have been many attempts over many years to try to regulate the profession of journalism, on the grounds that it may give offence to others, but all of these have failed. The laws against slander have been shown to be enough.

The freedom of speech that journalists enjoy, together with every other citizen, has clearly supported what democracy we have. The ability to question the actions of others always encourages good behaviour.

This can be very hard to do. There is a natural tendency by groups of people to exclude outsiders from the decision process, normally with the aim of efficiency, reinforced by the deluding thought that (we) specialists must know best. Self-contained groups like this, call them governments, can then become prey to skilful outsiders, say pressure groups, who offer their equally self-assured knowledge to help to reach conclusions.

So now step forward Sir Harold Evans. The setting

is the Banqueting House in Whitehall, rich with gilt, with a ceiling by Rubens and the memory, outside on the street, of the execution of Charles 1. And the Undercroft (not the Crypt, mind you), designed for drunken parties. Well, there we were, a choice collection of the high and low from the world of British media, to witness the launch of Sir Harold in his new career as the perhaps over-grandly titled editor in chief (meaning figurehead) of Reuters, the international news agency, via the staging of an impressive seminar on the state of the world's media. (I owe much of my data on media to the Reuters Institute Foundation.)

After the predictably defensive presentations (politicians were pressing on media at the time) came the eventual descent to the welcoming Undercroft and much good and bad behaviour. Anyone standing on the balcony and looking down at the throng below could not have missed the magnetic centre, move as it may. The centre was the presence of Sir Harold and his wife, whom many think of as the dual nationality Anglo-American royalty of Manhattan, being pressed by their many admirers.

Admirers for what reason? you may ask. Well, first, for some, is that the still active octogenarian Sir Harold (or Harold, or Harry) is 25 years older than his wife, even though, as she says 'As far as he is concerned I am still 22'. That was her age when they met. Next, because they are now as famous as each other in the world of media, while still managing a family life on both sides of the Atlantic in a profession not known for good marriages. Next because, considering their British origins, you would not otherwise imagine they had anything in common, with him as the proud son of a Welsh engine driver in north country Manchester and her, the daughter of an English film producer from the salubrious home counties.

More seriously perhaps, they are both admired because they are more or less equally famous for breaking the mould of journalism in the twentieth century, fuelled by furious early experiences of what many would consider to be bad behaviour, or at least of not observing convention. She organising strikes at school to earn the right to cleaner underwear. He winning fights for cleaner air in industrial northern England.

But Harry would have been best known to most in the Banqueting House as the twentieth century's most respected editor, notably as editor of the *Sunday Times* for fourteen years, during which time his determination to fight for good causes often found him successfully beating at the doors of convention and authority, all the way to the Court of Human Rights in Strasbourg, where he challenged the British government. Of course he was lucky to have had the support of a benevolent proprietor, in the shape of the Canadian born but Scots inclined Lord Thomson of Fleet at the *Sunday Times*, who provided the finance and the freedom to conduct long campaigns over many countries. These included the fight to ban thalidomide, an untested drug dispensed to pregnant mothers which had led to thousands of malformed births (no arms or legs or fingers) all over the world, but which for many years had been denied and concealed by companies and governments. Harry forced a change in the law that had prevented journalists from reporting court cases, so making such stories known. After a decade real compensation was paid, at least to those thalidomide victims in Britain. Other fights unmasked long entrenched Russian spies in the British establishment, crooked property developers and antique dealers and the right, ultimately, to publish the sensitive diaries of a former government minister.

I was occasionally recruited as a subeditor at weekends on the Insight pages of the *Sunday Times*, but Harry's addiction to detail often meant that the moment a page proof reached my desk he would be there, leaning over my shoulder, marking the copy for me. Despite, thus, my minor contribution, it was nevertheless a great experience, if only as a means of meeting most of the journalists who, at the time, were my heroes. They were all attracted to Harry. The important thing is that this insistence on revealing important secrets inspired a whole generation of reporters.

Lady Evans, otherwise known as Tina Brown, has also, ironically, been officially accepted into polite society by being royally awarded the title of Commander of the British Empire. Her commanding career began at St Anne's,

Oxford with writing for the university magazine *Isis*, the left wing *New Statesman* and the humorous weekly *Punch*. She earned a bachelor's degree in English literature. Other work landed the Catherine Packenham Award for the best journalist under 25. When she did reach 25 she became editor of *Tatler*, the glossy magazine for superior people, which set the tone for the rest of her career, continuously ever upwards. She also increased its circulation fourfold. As features editor there before her, at much the same age, I can see her point of view. Rich people, famous people, glamorous people can be attractive and, especially, aspirational. And aspiration brings rewards.

Tina's rewards began six years later with an invitation from Conde Nast to edit the then floundering *Vanity Fair* magazine, which she did for eight years in New York, increasing circulation from 200,000 to 1.2 million, followed by editing the rather more established *New Yorker* for the following six years. Again circulation showed improvement, including a rise in newsstand sales by 145 percent, but, despite shedding 79 editorial workers and engaging another 50, it never managed to move beyond being a costly publication, despite annual losses falling from $17m a year to a paltry $11m. (I am not aware of American editors in Britain, but there are many British editors in the USA.) All the same, Tina's fairly meteoric progression from one title to another produced the additional benefit of an impressive contacts book, both of persons of position and influence and of journalistic talent, starting (early) with Auberon Waugh, Martin Amis and Godfrey Smith, editor of the *Sunday Times* colour magazine; where, inevitably, she met her husband. Oh, and Harry was the most valued contributor to my quarterly journal, *Spokesman*.

# The ground is beginning to move

## EMMOTT, KENNEDY, PUTTNAM, BOOTHROYD

Democracy is a global label, but having unwritten rules does not help. In a recent book *The Fate of the West* by Bill Emmott, a former editor of *The Economist*, he puts it rather bluntly. 'In modern use the word democracy must carry little meaning beyond describing a mechanical process that can be used or misused at will.'

Surely democracy can mean only one thing: government by the people. Yet where does that happen? Clearly not in Britain. We have indirect democracy, in theory working through representatives, but it does not seem to be working. There is a rapidly growing absence of mandate. In the long term, voting turnout has fallen over the whole of the western world. The last international survey of public confidence in governments rated Britain as thirteenth in line, with a rating of 36.42 percent. Denmark came first, with 74.92 percent. Elections for mayors saw a slightly bigger turnout, showing a growing interest in local issues, otherwise people were never so disengaged with traditional politics and government. Only one in a hundred belongs to a party, while self-governing pressure groups are given ten times the cash than all the political parties together. Yet - with greater education and online information, few have been so well informed, and interest in issues is growing. The educational motivation is clear: first class degrees in the past five years have increased by fifty percent.

The benefits of public involvement are obvious. To see it in purely financial terms, those cantons in Switzerland with the most public initiatives (policies suggested by members of the public) also had the highest economic performance, while US states using public initiatives reported that the cost of public services were 20 percent lower than others.

In other surveys, good government has been voted the prime key to social happiness. It is certainly time to clear the air and to start all over again. Again to quote Bill Emmott: 'Britain is going to have to restore equality of voice by giving its political system at least as big a shake-up as Thatcher gave its economic system.'

Admittedly, politicians have tried. The lawyer Baroness Helena Kennedy chaired the Power Inquiry for The Rountree Trust, staging hundreds of meetings and consulting thousands of people and analysing the results for months, producing a detailed list of suggestions designed to re-engage the public in the way that the country is run. She said that in general 'people no longer want to join a party or get involved in formal politics' and that the solution is to download power by rebalancing the system towards the people'. She said citizens should be able to initiate laws and question politicians. The result was a stunning silence.

Lord Puttnam, a former colleague of mine, a film producer and a school governor, delivered a similar report to his peers which pointed out that society has changed, but Parliament has not.

The problem is that the present system leaves any decision on how to improve it with those we have put in charge, but their incentive to do so is small. So generally they don't. They think it might cancel their future. Usually only when they retire from Parliament do they care to admit the truth.

Take Tony Benn, perhaps in his day Britain's most admired government minister, who said he was giving up government for politics. Which he did, by making beautiful sounds. No longer bound by party loyalty, he could tour the country with his silver tongue to help promote a better world. The reaction from his former colleagues showed no more than amused disdain.

And take Betty Boothroyd, perhaps the most skilled Commons Speaker ever - and always the liveliest person in a room - who spelt out the issues to fellow members when she stood down from the chair. 'The level of cynicism about Parliament, and the accompanying alienation of many of the young from the democratic process, is troubling. It is an issue on which every member of the House should wish to reflect. It is our responsibility, each and every one of us, to do what we can to develop and build public trust and confidence.'

She quoted a report from the Select Committee on Public Administration, MPs from various parties, which pointed out that 'Debates on public policy increasingly take place only between professionals, without involving the public. Elites are seeking legitimation for their initiatives rather than a dialogue about what should or should not be done in the future. This causes resentment and probably leads to bad decisions. Involving the public has come to be seen as a problem to be managed, rather than a source to be used. While managing the problem produces an increase in obvious propaganda, which creates even more distrust.'

In terms of reaching a resolution Betty Boothroyd concluded that 'Polling people on their attitudes to democracy is pointless unless there is common agreement on the meaning of the word. Equally, polling people on their willingness to be publicly involved is pointless unless the value of that involvement is clear'.

The hunger for improvement is obvious. Nowadays we live in a world where daily everyone is making decisions of personal importance. We are comparing value, judging prices, designing and shaping our immediate surroundings by seeking advice and conducting research before we decide. It's not hard. We call it shopping. Meanwhile, others are spending more of our money, taken from what we pay in taxes, on equally important things like our health and education. There is clearly a disconnect. We are told that if we don't like the result of what others are doing for us, we can eventually elect others for the next five years. There is no guarantee the result will be better, but this is generally described as progress. Many find that hard to believe.

This does not matter only to national government. There are 19,000 politicians elected locally who share a similar blame.

An electoral commission ten years ago stressed that 'the system is close to breaking point' and that 'the most important thing is to put electors at the heart of decision making'. Soon after a reader of The Economist wrote to say that 'Electing politicians . . . to the status of leaders keeps the people in a state of permanent infancy . . . As any experienced parent will tell you, the best way to stop children from laying blame on others is to make them responsible for their own decisions, even if that means letting them make their own mistakes. It is the process of growing up and becoming adult. Give the kids a chance. Let them make their own choices'.

A government department, The Better Regulation Executive, has received a clear brief from the British public on how to improve the process of government, primarily by consulting before, not after. Not talking to, but with. Those steering the ship give the strong impression of waiting for the iceberg to hit.

# Now that the parties are over

## FACTIONALISM GOOD, OLIGARCHY BAD

**S**o why are political parties losing members? There was a certain logic in forming parties, to create majority factions to win votes in Parliament, when it started in Britain two centuries ago. With representative government, with gang against gang, it helped to overcome opposition, by force if not by argument. The trouble is that, once a gang is formed, it tends to need a controlling structure, which inevitably costs money.

Finance now comes out of our taxes, to pay for promotion, staff and postage, and free time on television when an election is near. About £25m for parties annually, plus £7.25m for the opposition in the Commons and £646,000 for the opposition in the Lords, to compensate for access to the machinery of government that the ruling party has. Small beer when compared with the national budget, but important all the same. The more parties, the more it costs us. And as more politicians come and go, they still expect their pensions. As you will see in a later section, none of this happens in Switzerland.

More dubiously, parties get dollops of cash from random people and organisations. Bernie Ecclestone gave Labour £1m, for instance. And what do they expect for that? One of the biggest of the political donors, Stuart Wheeler, described it as natural that people like him would get political influence. While life peer Michael Farmer admitted 'You cannot get away from the fact that the word 'peerage' is connected to large donations'.

Some eighty percent of the public believes that outside money interferes with government. Every political party has promised to 'address' it, both before and since the expenses scandal, but have yet to find a way. Does anyone paying taxes approve? Was anyone paying taxes consulted? The answer is a muffled silence.

The fundamental question, of course, is why have political parties anyway? As pressure groups they have agendas far from the public need, with items not on a public shopping list, partly because those same agendas are open to pressure from those with pockets that are deep enough to persuade. Meanwhile, loyalty to political parties between 1987 and 2010 fell from 46 to 36 percent. Leadership needs rethinking.

# The British birth

## GANDHI, ROUSSEAU AND LINCOLN

t could help to be clear on how we got our government. Most believe it evolved from Athens. Of course, that was twenty-five centuries ago and the world has changed a lot since then, so systems, naturally, have also changed, for the better or the worse.

Government certainly evolves. The Magna Carta in Britain removed government from monarchy. This was transferred to the House of Lords. These particular lords were self-appointed, as each of them had a private army. Later Oliver Cromwell restricted the Lords and real power moved to the House of Commoners, the better to represent the people and more easily reach agreement. Representatives would be elected by the public. But, still, the power to elect those representatives was for many years a minority sport. Only men with land and money could vote, which even as late as 1780 meant merely three percent of them. It took a hundred years more for all men to have a vote. Women had to wait much longer.

Yet though Parliament was meant to encourage agreement, it was not designed to deliver democracy. It was generally thought that affairs of state were best conducted as they were before, by those who could afford to work for nothing and had also learned to read. So the right to an opinion on who runs government has been widened only gradually. Now politicians get salaries, pensions and expenses, which opens the job to all who can read, but they still make decisions on running the country on behalf of their electors. This, still, is government for the people, but it certainly is not government by the people. What you do *for* me, *without* me, you do *to* me, said Gandhi.

So Britain has representative democracy, which has worked well enough for nearly three centuries, while political parties have lasted for two. And everyone aged at least eighteen has had equal voting rights since 1969, when the minimum age for women to vote was lowered from twenty-one. Adjustments have been made, eventually. But the world has changed much faster.

Rousseau said many years ago that representative democracy degraded humanity and also dishonoured the name of man. Not many chose to listen. All the same, interest in politics has strengthened - because of education and media - at least in specific issues. But this isn't just about words alone. It is about shaping the world we live in. Electing someone to do that for you, up to four years before the issues are known, seems naive and, frankly, foolish.

Abraham Lincoln is reported as saying that 'Government of the people, by the people, for the people, shall not perish from this earth'. Oops, it has already gone, on both sides of the Atlantic. Turnout for US local elections has fallen to an average of three percent. In some places in Britain it has dropped to ten.

# The Greek birth

ADVICE FROM SAMUEL BRITTAN

We should also be clear about the city state of Athens and what its example still has to offer. Its culture could not have sprung from a vacuum. Communal decisions on civic issues had been previously practiced in India. Nevertheless, to avoid fruitless argument, it helps to consider ancient Athens as a prototype for early democracy at the birth of present Europe. What democracy is not is control by one person. Nor is it control by force of arms. Neither is it control by pressure groups, either religious, commercial or political. Democracy should free every member of society to play a part in running their country, deciding, not just suggesting. Of course, if citizens decline to make decisions, they are obviously free in Britain to do so. Being forced by others to take a view is clearly not democracy.

So back to ancient Athens. Government consisted of three major platforms. The first was a general public assembly, of 6,000 men aged over 20, meeting generally ten times a year. Their names were drawn by lot. Their role was mainly to rule on new laws, although they could also make proposals. The agenda was published before the meeting. Speakers were heard both for and against. This favoured the common man. The second layer was a 500-member council, elected by members of the public assembly on the basis of their particular skills, which proposed legislation and appointed the executive. This favoured the elite. Finally, there were the public magistrates: 600 being chosen by lot, plus 100 elected on the basis of skill, all off them aged over 30. This mainly favoured the common man. (Now the only citizen power in Britain is the picking of juries at random.) Expenses only were paid to delegates. With few exceptions, all jobs were for a year. No-one could do the same job twice. Hence politics were open to everyone, but could not provide a career. A misuse of position within that timescale would obviously be difficult.

A distinctive part of the Athenian system was the drawing of lots to select representatives. To quote Aristotle: 'The basis of a democratic state is liberty. One principle of liberty is for all to rule and to be ruled in turn'. This may not have been a perfect system, but it worked well enough for nearly two hundred years, until it was destroyed by invading armies, but it was judged to have been better than previous systems on the grounds that it ensured a balance between two interests, the elite and the common man.

Choosing officials only at random could possibly lead to incompetence, but if chosen only by election it could lead to impotence. It certainly had Aristotle's approval: 'When the people as a body have sovereign power, it is a democracy. When sovereign power in the hands of a part of the people, it is an aristocracy'. Combining both, he thought, was best.

This general format was adopted by others. First by other city states in the region, Florence, Venice, Pisa and so on, then later in countries such as Germany and Spain. The drawing of lots to appoint governors, albeit from a limited list, was still in use in the twentieth century in countries such as San Marino.

The economic journalist Samuel Brittan is well worth quoting: 'Most of the political text books say that direct democracy on the Greek pattern is impossible in a large modern state. But it is becoming more possible every day. Modern electronics brings the prospect of continuing referenda on every subject under the sun on the local, national and international levels nearer and nearer. This aside from the use or misuse that politicians make of focus groups. What then is wrong with the idea of continuous voting on one subject after another? To say that it may have worked in the special case of Switzerland does not dispose of the issue. This is an easy question to answer for either conservative authoritarians who are happy to assert that people do not know their own interests and that either traditional rulers or scientific experts know them better. It is also easy for Marxists who believe that people are affected by "false consciousness" and that their interests must be interpreted by a proletarian vanguard.'

It is fair to mention that a major incentive for the Athenian elite to share power with the public was the continual threat of external attack, so encouraging new recruits for the military. Now, for most countries, the motivation is not from without, but within.

# On a Swiss roll

OTHERS CAN SOMETIMES KNOW BEST

So now back to my friend Teresa in Basle. And yes, I agree that the Swiss are different, as Alastair Burnet insisted. But, then, what nation isn't? Britain is surrounded by sea, which has turned us into an island race, intuitively at least. (Continent cut off by fog, etc.) Switzerland has some notable mountains, which have always discouraged invaders. This has made it effectively an island in the centre of a land mass. Britain has had a few civil wars, religious conflicts and worker revolts. It has also managed to get nations together to form a single state. Remarkably, so has Switzerland. England's hero, St George, was Turkish. Switzerland has William Tell, who is now believed to have been Danish. Both countries are multi-religious and multi-lingual but the devil for both is always a foreigner. (Bearing in mind that those most against foreigners are mainly also those who feel they have no control over their world.) Yet both countries have flourished by admitting foreigners with strong ambition and skills.

But there certainly are differences. From early years Britain has centralised the state, while Switzerland has generally not: the driving force there has come from farmers, whose aim was to guard their land from neighbours. Local interests must always come first. The

Swiss also resisted control by the church, by rich landlords and political movements. Napoleon conquered the country but not their minds. Farmers also had a second career, as soldiers for hire to foreign armies - the remainder of which now guard the Pope. The result was the creation of local cantons, which have always managed to resist domination by the Swiss Confederation.

There are two parliamentary bodies, the federal council, elected by the federal assembly, and the council of states, modelled on the US senate to represent the cantons. Sometimes both sit together for constitutional issues. The job of president is filled in turn by each of the seven government ministers, but only for a year at a time, hence few Swiss can name their leader.

Britain also had an element of strong local government, at least until the 19th century, but since then their powers have been reduced, so that now local government is 70 percent reliant on the central state for funding and is sensitive to central guidance. The twenty-five Swiss cantons are finally responsible for delivering all public policies, which they do with a deal of discretion.

An important issue is the funding of politics. Apart from allowances for politicians, political parties get no public money, nor do campaigners for referenda. This can mean that big money interests - chemical companies come to mind, as well as groups of employers and workers - can have a major influence.

But Switzerland is not a direct democracy, despite what many say. Nobody is asked to vote every week, but possibly once a month. It is best described as an inclusive democracy where the public have the power of veto. There are still elected representatives who deal with detail and initiate laws and take direct action at times of need, but do not do it as a full-time job. This keeps their feet on the ground. The public can also initiate laws, in the form of amendments to the constitution, providing there is enough support. This means that many laws are rejected, which at least ensures that those that get through are likely to be effective. Of the hundreds of laws passed annually in Britain most disappear from view.

Despite little more than five percent of Swiss citizens' initiatives becoming law, the overall effect of campaigning increases the willingness of politicians to embrace unexpected points of view. They can see how the wind is blowing, or not.

Turnout for elections is no bigger than Britain's, but that's because interest in the issues varies. Electors vote only when they have concern. Yet a constant truth is that understanding of the issues is impressive. Before elections each citizen gets a printed briefing, authored by the government and the proposing body, in time for public discussion and media scrutiny.

Authentication of votes is greater than in Britain, as everyone must register their residential address within two weeks of moving in, so official documents can be delivered and identities confirmed. Most votes are returned by post and checked before registration. This compares with the bizarre British Brexit, a referendum called without explanation and no independent summary of possible outcomes. Was the Electoral Commission sleeping?

Politicians are still effective in raising issues and scrutinising government. In Britain we have select committees that concentrate mainly on the delivery of policy after legislation is passed, but the Swiss committees do most of their work on shaping legislation for parliament before it is shown to the public. This echoes the system that Harold Macmillan had in mind for Britain with the National Economic Development Council, which was killed off by Margaret Thatcher.

The nine Swiss committees work in private, so are able to consider extreme opinions without encouraging public exposure. National Council committees have 25 members, in the Council of States they have 13 members. They normally meet for a day or two between parliamentary assemblies. Once they agree on a policy they pass it on to the appropriate house and issue a public statement. This leaves less scope for grandstanding. Public debates are more collaborative.

It is a gradual process, which means that legislation can take seven years to complete for really controversial issues. But compared with the fifty years in Britain it has taken to approve an extension to Heathrow and the twenty-three years for the Channel Tunnel it can be seen as better.

The European Union presents the Swiss with problems much like those of Britain's. A referendum in 2014 ruled against the free movement of people (in reaction to 24% of population being foreign), although the central government had been trying for years to negotiate free trade. In the event, in December 2016, the government overruled the vote, in order to do better business with the EU. Which pleased big companies but made the public furious. The next general election will tell.

A distinct feature of the Swiss system is the courts. Unlike anywhere else in Europe, judges are appointed by the federal council, in other words the government. This means that government decisions are never expected to be overturned by the courts. The Swiss say this does not worry them, because the public can intervene at many levels of national government. Others would say that some appointments call for specialist knowledge. The subject for a referendum, perhaps.

# What we want

## ON NO, NOT MORE POLITICS

**I**t could be useful take a look at what the British public says it wants. Of course this may be breaking a law, but I think it is a chance worth taking. The Better Regulation Executive surveyed opinion on consultations by government. They took the views of people in three disparate towns, selected as to be representative of age and level of involvement in government. The survey team started by telling participants that the government normally has 600 consultations every year, including, amazingly, the Ministry of Defence. This surprised every participant but two, as nobody else had heard of them. But, all the same, participants liked the idea and soon came up with some clear ideas on how they should be conducted.

1 - Everyone should know about each consultation, even if they chose to not respond.

2 - Avoid dealing only with pressure groups.

3 - Ensure consultations are known to those most affected.

4 - Always use more than print media.

5 - Don't consult during holidays or without allowing time for reaction.

6 - Don't ask questions without optional answers, plus clear opinions from specialists.

7 - Don't make decisions without considering reaction.

8 - Don't act on decisions without giving a reason and allowing more reaction.

Why nobody has thought to act on this is puzzling, and suspicious. Undoubtedly, a seed had been planted for ways to improve participation in government. Obviously the seed was not watered. Brexit, of course, was a perfect example of how not to consult the public.

The World Forum for Democracy meets in Strasbourg every year and its theme for 2017 is the growing disconnect between citizens and elites; as it has been, more or less, in every other year. There have been many surveys conducted on politics, but they have concentrated on just two areas: Parliament and elections. This is easiest to do, as both exist - although growing less attractive. Hence the desire of Britons for a different electoral system has grown from 27 percent in 2011 to 45 percent in 2015. But very much harder to define are ideas for a better and closer government. On the other hand, it could be useful to compare these thoughts with those of a specialist. Mark Thompson was director general of the BBC and former chief executive of Channel Four Television who progressed to CEO of the *New York Times*. Many might remember his BBC salary of £834,000 but refusal to waste money on shoes or haircut, yet a pause between jobs when he lectured at Oxford led to his seminal book *Enough Said*. He clearly feels strongly about the lack of engagement between government and the people, for instance quoting Gallop polls of 1944 and 2014 which show that the proportion of people thinking that politicians put the nation before other interests has fallen from 36 to 10 percent.

Thompson believes that what this demonstrates is a failure of the language of politics. He says that people are keen to engage, as shown by their love of social media. The solution he suggests is better education, of politicians, media and the public. They all need a better grasp of rhetoric, he says.

Without denying that education has an important role, this is a process that would take many years. Surely, better to improve the design of policy, so to better involve the public.

The greatest dangers in Britain are those closest to us. Reforming the welfare state is urgent. Maintaining the NHS and pensions will be hard to achieve without general agreement, as somebody has to pay for them. It is better if they do that willingly.

# The Spedan solution

## AN ANSWER IN THE HIGH STREET

have been told by a number of government ministers that they would like to run their departments as efficiently as the John Lewis partnership. Of course we are used to politicians making promises that they don't deliver, either because they can't or won't, but that should not kill a good idea that still deserves consideration. Nevertheless, it calls for understanding of how the idea could be adopted.

The John Lewis group has a constitution that owes its life to a horse. John Spedan Lewis was the eldest son of John Lewis, the man who started the store in Oxford Street, in the retail heart of London. At nineteen he became a junior director and seemed destined for a future as his father's son. Until he was suddenly thrown from a horse and had to spend time on his back recovering. As young men very often do, he thought deeply about his future.

His father seemed to work night and day and made a good living from doing deals, while making sure that no money was wasted on spending. As a director Spedan knew that, as a result of that, the profit (their income) was much greater than the total pay of the three hundred staff, whose wages at the lowest level put extra spending beyond their means, and especially not on horses. He failed to convince his father to change. He argued for a fairer share of profits, as well as sharing control of the business with everyone who worked for it. Then his mother died and his father softened, at least as far as allowing Spedan to experiment with Peter Jones, their second store. In the in event, the gamble paid off. Peter Jones had been losing money anyway, so a mistake would have not looked so bad.

Of course, the change was not a gamble, but the result of careful thought and the construction of a management system for the whole of the group still in use today. The motivation behind the plan was to get all workers employed in the business to think of it as their personal property. In this way they would be more likely to think positively of what they did, as well as ensuring that pay for work was justified by input. Pay rates were decided by the workers.

The management system allowed staff, called partners, to be involved in decisions in a variety of ways. They would help appoint the various managers. They could vote to remove ineffective staff, even up to the highest level. At the same time, managers presented plans with their rationale, while the chairman retained the power of veto on ideas that seemed unsafe. The chairman was the chief executive. Essential to success was communication, ensuring that every partner could access basic information. Spedan launched *The Gazette* to inform every partner, staffed from the start with people who were skilled in explaining business issues.

Most importantly in financial terms, there were no investors or external shareholders, as the business was a partnership. After a primary period of employment, every worker became a partner, so shared the annual profits.

At the time of writing, the group has 45 stores including Waitrose food shops and 90,000 partners. Profits in 2016 of £488.2m meant a 6 percent profit share for partners, equal to three weeks pay.

Spedan's initiative had much to do with his sympathy with the workers of his father's day, firmly believing that, with people starving, no-one should be a millionaire. At the same time, he believed that capitalism could produce the best kind of life for all. He may not at first have realised that, with happier workers, the mood would also energise customers. And in every business, as everyone knows, the customer is king. London.

Applying this principle to the practice of government should not be all that difficult. The aim is maximising involvement. The mechanism for enabling involvement might not be very far removed from that of ancient Athens.

To quote Bill Emmott of *The Economist* again: 'Democracy powered by the internet and the smart phone . . . might be imagined to work better and better all the time, with an inbuilt mechanism for ensuring that one man, one vote really does bring equality of influence. Well, it is a nice idea, and perhaps one day it will happen. But for the time being, there is no sign of it'.

I am dedicating this book to my good friend Gaziza, studying management at MIT and Harvard. She can put this into action.

Did anyone mention blockchain?

Laurie Lee and Sarah Cooper off to Spain

Malcom Muggeridge less than reverend

A J P Taylor

Bertrand Russell

Alastair Burnet

David English

Joyce Grenfell

Alistair Cooke

Paul Foot

Edward Mortimer

David Puttnam

Peter Preston

David Frost

Gerry Mansell

Norman Macrae

Bob Guccioni

Brendan Bracken

Mark Starowicz

Quentin Peel

Bridget Kendall

Mr and Mrs Evans

APPENDIX

# **The birth of Brexit**

## THE RESULT OF A MISSING STRATEGY

I have a confession to make. For over two decades I was the executive secretary of the British section of the Association of European Journalists. And I basically failed.

It was our job to not only campaign for a free media, but also to help deepen the understanding of European affairs among the general public, and to inform about the work of European institutions. However, we found it impossible, over many years, to communicate the essential truth about the European project to the continent's population, not because of lack of effort, but simply through lack of opportunity.

It was not just a failure on my part, but on the part of those behind that project. The politicians who have been, they think, running Europe have admittedly been steering the institutions of Europe but not the people. Those citizens and voters have discovered only what had been decided on their behalf long after the commitment had been made and when, therefore, that knowledge was of no practical use to them. Recounting history is not news. Making history is.

Let me go back to 1992, when the AEJ took over two central London hotels and the QEII Conference Centre in order to stage its annual conference. Over 400 journalists from all over Europe, either from nations already members of the EU or else expecting to become members, gathered together to listen to over 100 speakers on every possible aspect of civic co-operation. There were three days of talks, many lunches, many dinners. This was largely funded by tax payers.

The one problem that was continuously raised and put to the various EU officials was lack of information: we needed to know what was going on. In effect, we were brushed aside. We would know when the time was right, we were told. This, in effect, meant that we would be told when all the differences had been resolved and the final agreements had been made. The obvious fact that this was too late to be of any interest or practical use was either never heard or, more likely, ignored.

Since then, every morning in Brussels, a press conference has been staged to supply journalists with similarly redundant information, which is duly recorded and passed to editors, who normally put it straight in the bin.

Twenty-four years after the London meeting, the majority of Britons gave up trying to understand and gladly threw in the towel. Not, I suggest, as a token of rejection, but as a simple act of frustration. In effect, in my opinion, few voted either for or against the EU, as few even knew what it did. Most voted against a political system that took no notice of them. A senior director I know in the Commission sent me an email after the vote almost stained with tears. "How could people as intelligent as the British make such a really stupid decision?" I told her not to take it personally, it was the politicians' fault, not hers.

All of this is succinctly demonstrated in an impressive and very readable book published just days before the referendum: *The European Union: a citizen's guide* by a Cambridge University lecturer, Chris Bickerton.

Policy making behind closed doors is at the core of it. Understandable in the early days of the arcane European Coal and Steel Community, the habit of government officers talking only to other government officers has persisted right through to the current era when what is now the European Union has the ability to influence nearly every aspect of our lives. Politicians, who have seen this happen, have found it easy to allow it to happen, as it makes their work so very much easier. And so the habit has become ingrained with politicians of every nation to make agreements with other nations, but to claim to their voters that the final result was nothing to do with them. As nobody else is in the room whenever deals are being done there can be no explanation or denial. The miasma of conflicting rumours from anonymous sources from many nations makes the fog much thicker and nastier.

It is not that the Commission has not tried hard. Its president (one of four in the system) has had long talks with communication advisers to at least understand how others work. But the power to correct is not his. Of course, wild media loves its fantasies, ranging from the banning of bent bananas to restricting the size of vacuum cleaners. But Commission reaction in the form of denials has just as much value as any denial: the lady plainly protests too much, so the story probably has to be true.

When Michael Heseltine lunched with the AEJ at the time when he was hoping to unseat Margaret Thatcher his reaction to all the leaks from Brussels was to throw up his hands in exasperation. "Brussels leaks like a sieve" he said. But possibly he had never worked there, so had never realised why. A recent report from the Reuters Institute (*Reporting the EU* by John Lloyd and Cristina Marconi) spells out how much EU officials have earnestly tried to connect with the world.

The annual budget for communication was Euro 246m, with the Parliament spending Euro 21m and the Council Euro 10.4m. If this seems like a lot of money, it is. However, this is largely because the Commission and the Council each employs about 100 spokesmen, and the Parliament 86. But on top of that MEPs employ about 751, on either a full or part time basis. One might think this makes the Pentagon security leaks look trivial; how can information be sensibly managed with so many tempted to target new jobs or do favours for newly made friends?

But the leaking does not stop there, unfortunately. The real briefing on what may or may not be happening is not in the hands of the supposedly non-political Commissioners or their civil servants, but in the hands of the many national political leaders who each give their version of the truth, openly or furtively, to their own national audiences. The party line comes first, of course.

Expecting journalists to sort this out, when the most influential media is television, where the space for words is conditioned by sound bites, is tempting but optimistic.

The wider message from this deeply ingrained demonstration of political incompetence is that it has become a world-wide practice, of not informing and not involving electors in fundamental issues that affect them at a time when it would be of most value. Which clearly explains why an ever better educated and more ambitious public has become increasingly disaffected with politicians and political systems.

The main problem with Chris Bickerton's book is that it was published too late to effect the referendum. Perhaps, instead, together with the Reuters report, it could be put at the top of reading lists for politicians on their next break. Even on continental beaches.

**This was written for *The New European*, just after the vote on Brexit.**

Other books by

Kevin d'Arcy

*The voice of the brain of Britain*

*Who's in charge here?*

*London's 2nd city*

All published by

Rajah Books